ALEXANDRE DUMAS

THE LADY OF THE CAMELLIAS

Translated by Edmund Gosse

ALAN SUTTON
1986

Alan Sutton Publishing Limited
30 Brunswick Road
Gloucester GL1 1JJ

This translation first published 1902

British Library Cataloguing in Publication Data

Dumas, Alexandre, *1824–1895*
    The lady of the camellias.
    I. Title II. Gosse, Edmund III. La dame aux
camelias. *English*
    843'.8[F]   PQ2231.D32

    ISBN 0-86299-264-8

Cover picture: detail from Self-Portrait *by*
Rolinda Sharples.
City of Bristol Museum and Art Gallery.

Typesetting and origination by
Alan Sutton Publishing Limited.
Photoset Bembo 9/10.
Printed in Great Britain
by The Guernsey Press Company Limited,
Guernsey, Channel Islands.

BIOGRAPHICAL NOTE

There are two French writers by the name of Alexandre Dumas. The elder wrote plays and novels, and was an outstanding character in French Bohemian society. The most well-known works of his prodigious output are *The Three Musketeers* and *The Count of Monte Cristo*. The younger, his son, is remembered more for his skills as a dramatist than as a novelist. He too was a prominent figure in Parisian society, but was more conservative and moral than his profligate father.

Alexandre Dumas *fils* was born on 27th July 1824 when his father, grandson of a French plantation owner and a Negro slave, was in his early twenties and his mother, Catherine Lebay, some years older. They were not married and lived together for only a short time after the birth of their child. Catherine, a competent dressmaker, intelligent but un-educated, provided her son with a secure and loving home during his early childhood. His father maintained an interest in the child, later sending him to the boarding school of his friend, Goubaux, a dramatist and educationalist. Alexandre was very unhappy there as he describes in his semi-autobiographical novel, *L'Affaire Clemenceau* (1866). He suffered ignominiously because of his illegitimacy, his father's notorious prodigality and his undisguised affection for his mother. Eventually his father realized that the boy was unhappy to the point of illness and moved him to another school, where he rapidly recovered both emotionally and physically. The contrast of the security he had experienced with his mother and the misery he had suffered on account of his father's waywardness was to awaken in him a serious and questioning attitude towards social and moral responsibilities.

On leaving school in 1840, Alexandre went to live with his father, who was reaching the height of his literary fame. He was treated with great generosity and launched into a life of dissipation. Although Alexandre became his father's best friend, he shows his later maturity when he writes:

When I was eighteen his exuberance took charge of my youth and my curiosity and we set out together in quest of amusement in society – shocking, wasn't it? But one can observe and store up experiences everywhere; and it may be that we found a richer field of observation and experience in the resorts in which we diverted ourselves than we should have found in any ponderous philosophical tomes.

(preface to *La Femme de Claude*)

It was during these years that Dumas became the acquaintance and then the lover of a well-known courtesan, Marie Dupleissis. Born Alphonsine Plessis, she had come to Paris as a young, uneducated and penniless country girl and had made her way socially and financially by becoming mistress first of a restauranteur, then of minor nobility, and finally of the Duc de Guiche. A *femme entretenue* to a number of men, she welcomed, for a while, an *affaire du cœur* and the passionate love of a goodlooking and lively young man; but in 1846 the relationship came to an end. Six months later, Marie Dupleissis, who always wore white camellias, died of tuberculosis at the age of twenty-three. The sale of her effects marked the climax of popular interest in the beautiful young woman and provided the opening scene for the novel which was to lead to her immortalization as *La Dame aux Camélias*.

Since leaving school, Dumas had been writing indifferent poetry. In 1847 he completed his first novel, *Les Aventures de Quatre Femmes et d'un Perroquet*, but this work was of no great merit and provided little towards settling the author's accumulating debts. The success of his second novel, *La Dame aux Camélias*, however, was sensational. The life of Marie Dupleissis had fascinated Paris society and a book written by a former lover had instant appeal. Dumas romanticized their love, the characters involved and the tragic outcome, but he recaptured the intensity of his own love in the love of Armand Duval, thus giving the novel some literary worth. It was written in three weeks and published in 1848. The following year Dumas adapted the novel for the stage. However, it was three years before the censors would allow its performance. During that time Dumas wrote a number of mediocre novels; it was the production of *La Dame aux*

Camélias at the Vaudeville in 1852 which finally established him as a man of letters. The play was an instant success, its romantic sentiments bringing tears to all but the most cynical. It captured the imagination of Verdi, who, the following year, crystallized the love of Armand and Marguerite, renamed Violetta, in the passionate music of *La Traviata*.

Dumas, in the mean time, had fallen in love with a Russian countess, whom he pursued to Russia. The affair came to nought, but provided material for his next novel/play, *Diane de Lys*. He travelled round Europe with his father, gaining experience, writing and thinking more deeply than his father ever would about social and moral problems. In 1885 his first distinctive play appeared, called *Le Demi-Monde*, the title a term invented by Dumas. It was set in a half-world of socially unacceptable women separated from their husbands or maintained by married men, and was concerned with the effects of prostitution on marriage. It was the first *drame-à-thèse*, a play about a social problem, with the author's attitude expressed by the voice of the *raisonneur*. This technique and the unsentimental moralizing tone was to become the mark of the younger Dumas' work, and culminated in *Les Idées de Madame Aubray*, first performed in 1867.

As the father grew old and decadent, the son was emerging as a reputable and influential figure in Paris society. He married the Princess Narishkine, a Russian, and had two daughters. Later he lived apart from his wife, but the alliance provided a façade of respectability. Dumas had many ideas and theories about the irregularities of marriage and the role of women, which were not consistent, but were delivered with confidence and aplomb in his plays and essays and in the many prefaces he wrote to his works. He was highly-strung, and suffered at least two nervous breakdowns, one in his late teens, which took the form of a religious mania, and another in his mid-forties. His nervous tension is reflected in the melodramatic and exaggerated style sometimes adopted by the writer, as, for example, in *L'Affaire Clemenceau*, and in his tirade against Paris in an essay of 1870.

In 1875 he was made a member of the Academie Française, in appreciation of his contribution to French literature and in recognition of his moral worth. He was one of the most important dramatists of the nineteenth century, bringing back to the French stage a sense of reality, as well as a moral awareness. He took an active part in theatre life: in 1878 he finished and produced his father's play, *Joseph Balsamo*. Sarah Bernhardt often acted in his plays, and Dumas was so moved by her performance in a revival of *La Dame aux Camélias* in 1884 that he gave her an early edition of the novel, with a letter, retrieved in a sale, which he had written to Marie Dupleissis at the end of their romance, forty years earlier:

My dear Marie,

I am neither rich enough to love you in the way in which I should wish nor poor enough to be your lover on the terms which you propose. So let us both forget – you a name which must be very nearly indifferent to you – I a happiness which has become impossible for me.

It is superfluous for me to tell you how sorry I am, for you know how much I love you. Goodbye, then. You have too tender a heart not to understand why I am writing this letter and too much intelligence not to forgive me for writing it.

Mille souvenirs.

A.D.

His plays were generally considered too outrageous for English Victorian society, but his last play, *Francillon*, was adapted by H.A. Jones and caused a considerable stir when it was first performed in London. His *Théâtre Complet* appeared in eight volumes in 1893. In 1878–9 he published *Entr'actes*, three volumes of essays on literary, theatrical and social topics. Recognized as an authoritative member of society, he published two pamphlets on divorce and prostitution, which were effective in the revision of the French marriage laws.

In 1895 Madame Dumas died, and Dumas, at the age of seventy-one, married Madame Regnier de la Brise, whom he had loved for many years. Later that year he became ill with meningitis, and died on 27th November. Many people attended the funeral of one of the great literary figures of the century at the cemetery of Montmartre.

SHEILA MICHELL

CHAPTER I

In my opinion, it is impossible to create characters until one has spent a long time in studying men, as it is impossible to speak a language until it has been seriously acquired. Not being old enough to invent, I content myself with narrating, and I beg the reader to assure himself of the truth of a story in which all the characters, with the exception of the heroine, are still alive. Eye-witnesses of the greater part of the facts which I have collected are to be found in Paris, and I might call upon them to confirm me if my testimony is not enough. And, thanks to a particular circumstance, I alone can write these things, for I alone am able to give the final details, without which it would have been impossible to make the story at once interesting and complete.

This is how these details came to my knowledge. On the 12th March, 1847, I saw in the Rue Lafitte a great yellow placard announcing a sale of furniture and curiosities. The sale was to take place on account of the death of the owner. The owner's name was not mentioned, but the sale was to be held at 9, Rue d'Antin, on the 16th, from 12 to 5. The placard further announced that the rooms and furniture could be seen on the 13th and 14th.

I have always been very fond of curiosities, and I made up my mind not to miss the occasion, if not of buying some, at all events of seeing them. Next day I called at 9, Rue d'Antin.

It was early in the day, and yet there were already a number of visitors, both men and women, and the women, though they were dressed in cashmere and velvet, and had their carriages waiting for them at the door, gazed with aston-ishment and admiration at the luxury which they saw before them.

I was not long in discovering the reason of this aston-ishment and admiration, for, having begun to examine things a little carefully, I discovered without difficulty that I was in

1

the house of a kept woman. Now, if there is one thing which women in society would like to see (and there were society women there), it is the home of those women whose carriages splash their own carriages day by day, who, like them, side by side with them, have their boxes at the Opera and at the Italiens, and who parade in Paris the opulent insolence of their beauty, their diamonds, and their scandal.

This one was dead, so the most virtuous of women could enter even her bedroom. Death had purified the air of this abode of splendid foulness, and if more excuse were needed, they had the excuse that they had merely come to a sale, they knew not whose. They had read the placards, they wished to see what the placards had announced, and to make their choice beforehand. What could be more natural? Yet, all the same, in the midst of all these beautiful things, they could not help looking about for some traces of this courtesan's life, of which they had heard, no doubt, strange enough stories.

Unfortunately the mystery had vanished with the goddess, and, for all their endeavours, they discovered only what was on sale since the owner's decease, and nothing of what had been on sale during her lifetime. For the rest, there were plenty of things worth buying. The furniture was superb; there were rosewood and buhl cabinets and tables, Sèvres and Chinese vases, Saxe statuettes, satin, velvet, lace; there was nothing lacking.

I sauntered through the rooms, following the inquisitive ladies of distinction. They entered a room with Persian hangings, and I was just going to enter in turn, when they came out again almost immediately, smiling, and as if ashamed of their own curiosity. I was all the more eager to see the room. It was the dressing-room laid out with all the articles of toilet, in which the dead woman's extravagance seemed to be seen at its height.

On a large table against the wall, a table three feet in width and six in length, glittered all the treasures of Aucoc and Odiot. It was a magnificent collection, and there was not one of those thousand little things so necessary to the toilet of a woman of the kind which was not in gold or silver. Such a collection could only have been got together little by little, and the same lover had certainly not begun and ended it.

Not being shocked at the sight of a kept woman's dressing-room, I amused myself with examining every detail, and I discovered that these magnificently chiselled objects bore different initials and different coronets. I looked at one after another, each recalling a separate shame, and I said that God had been merciful to the poor child, in not having left her to pay the ordinary penalty, but rather to die in the midst of her beauty and luxury, before the coming of old age, the courtesan's first death.

Is there anything sadder in the world than the old age of vice, especially in woman? She preserves no dignity, she inspires no interest. The everlasting repentance, not of the evil ways followed, but of the plans that have miscarried, the money that has been spent in vain, is as saddening a thing as one can well meet with. I knew an aged woman who had once been 'gay', whose only link with the past was a daughter almost as beautiful as she herself had been. This poor creature to whom her mother had never said, 'You are my child,' except to bid her nourish her old age as she herself had nourished her youth, was called Louise, and, being obedient to her mother, she abandoned herself without volition, without passion, without pleasure, as she would have worked at any other profession that might have been taught her.

The constant sight of dissipation, precocious dissipation, in addition to her constant sickly state, had extinguished in her mind all knowledge of good and evil that God had perhaps given her, but that no one had ever thought of developing. I shall always remember her, as she passed along the boulevards almost every day at the same hour, accompanied by her mother as assiduously as a real mother might have accompanied her daughter. I was very young then, and ready to accept for myself the easy morality of the age. I remember, however, the contempt and disgust which awoke in me at the sight of this scandalous chaperoning. Her face, too, was inexpressibly virginal in its expression of innocence and of melancholy suffering. She was like a figure of Resignation.

One day the girl's face was transfigured. In the midst of all the debauches mapped out by her mother, it seemed to her as if God had left over for her one happiness. And why indeed should God, who had made her without strength, have left her without consolation, under the sorrowful burden of her life? One day, then, she realized that she was to have a child, and all that remained to her of chastity leaped for joy. The soul has strange refuges. Louise ran to tell the good news to her mother. It is a shameful thing to speak of, but we are not telling tales of pleasant sins; we are telling of true facts, which it would be better, no doubt, to pass over in silence, if we did not believe that it is needful from time to time to reveal the martyrdom of those who are condemned without hearing, scorned without judging; shameful it is, but this mother answered the daughter that they had already scarce enough for two, and would certainly not have enough for three; that such children are useless, and a lying-in is so much time lost.

Next day a midwife, of whom all we will say is that she was a friend of the mother, visited Louise, who remained in bed for a few days, and then got up paler and feebler than before.

Three months afterward a man took pity on her and tried to heal her, morally and physically; but the last shock had been too violent, and Louise died of it. The mother still lives. How? God knows.

This story returned to my mind while I looked at the silver toilet things, and a certain space of time must have elapsed during these reflections, for no one was inside the room but myself and an attendant, who, standing near the door, was carefully watching me to see that I did not pocket anything.

I went up to the man, to whom I was causing so much anxiety. 'Sir,' I said, 'can you tell me the name of the person who formerly lived here?'

'Mademoiselle Marguerite Gautier.'

I knew her by name and sight.

'What!' I said to the attendant; 'Marguerite Gautier is dead?'

'Yes, sir.'

'When did she die?'

'Three weeks ago, I believe.'

'And why are the rooms on view?'

'The creditors believe that it will send up the prices. People can see beforehand the effect of the things; you see, that induces them to buy.'

'She was in debt, then?'

'To some extent, sir.'

'But the sale will cover it?'

'And more too.'

'Who will get what remains over?'

'Her family.'

'She had a family?'

'It seems so.'

'Thanks.'

The attendant, reassured as to my intentions, touched his hat, and I went out.

'Poor girl!' I said to myself as I returned home, 'she must have had a sad death, for, in her world, one has friends only when one is perfectly well.' And in spite of myself I began to feel melancholy over the fate of Marguerite Gautier.

It will seem absurd to many people, but I have an unbounded sympathy for women of this kind, and I do not think it necessary to apologize for such sympathy.

One day, as I was going to the Prefecture for a passport, I saw in one of the neighbouring streets a poor girl who was being marched along by two policemen. I do not know what was the matter. All I know is that she was weeping bitterly as she kissed an infant only a few months old, from whom her arrest was to separate her. Since that day I have never dared to despise a woman at first sight.

CHAPTER II

The sale was to take place on the 16th. A day's interval had been left between the visiting days and the sale, in order to give time for taking down the hangings, curtains, etc.

I had just returned from abroad. It was natural that I had not heard of Marguerite's death among the pieces of news which one's friends always tell on returning after an absence. Marguerite was a pretty woman; but though the life of such women makes sensation enough, their death makes very little. They are suns which set as they rose, unobserved. Their death, when they die young, is heard of by all their lovers at the same moment, for in Paris almost all the lovers of a well-known woman are friends. A few recollections are exchanged, and everybody's life goes on as if the incident had never occurred, without so much as a tear.

Nowadays, at twenty-five, tears have become so rare a thing that they are not to be squandered indiscriminately. It is the most that can be expected if the parents who pay for being wept over are wept over in return for the price they pay.

As for me, though my initials did not occur on any of Marguerite's belongings, that instinctive indulgence, that natural pity that I have already confessed set me thinking over her death, more perhaps than it was worth thinking over. I remembered having often met Marguerite in the Bois, where she went regularly every day in a little blue coupé drawn by two magnificent bays, and I had noticed in her a distinction quite apart from other women of her kind, a distinction which was enhanced by a really exceptional beauty.

These unfortunate creatures whenever they go out are always accompanied by somebody or other. As no man cares to make himself conspicuous by being seen in their company, and as they are afraid of solitude, they take with them either those who are not well enough off to have a carriage, or one or another of these elegant, ancient ladies, whose elegance is a little inexplicable, and to whom one can always go for information in regard to the women whom they accompany.

In Marguerite's case it was quite different. She was always alone when she drove in the Champs-Élysées, lying back in her carriage as much as possible, dressed in furs in winter, and in summer wearing very simple dresses; and though she often passed people whom she knew, her smile, when she chose to smile, was seen only by them, and a duchess might have smiled in just such a manner. She did not drive to and fro like the others, from the Rond-Point to the end of the Champs-Élysées. She drove straight to the Bois. There she left her carriage, walked for an hour, returned to her carriage, and drove rapidly home.

All these circumstances which I had so often witnessed came back to my memory, and I regretted her death as one might regret the destruction of a beautiful work of art.

It was impossible to see more charm in beauty than in that of Marguerite. Excessively tall and thin, she had in the fullest degree the art of repairing this oversight of Nature by the mere arrangement of the things she wore. Her cashmere reached to the ground, and showed on each side the large flounces of a silk dress, and the heavy muff which she held pressed against her bosom was surrounded by such cunningly arranged folds that the eye, however exacting, could find no fault with the contour of the lines. Her head, a marvel, was the object of the most coquettish care. It was small, and her mother, as Musset would say, seemed to have made it so in order to make it with care.

Set, in an oval of indescribable grace, two black eyes, surmounted by eyebrows of so pure a curve that they seemed as if painted; veil these eyes with lovely lashes, which, when drooped, cast their shadow on the rosy hue of the cheeks; trace a delicate, straight nose, the nostrils a little open, in an ardent aspiration toward the life of the senses; design a regular mouth, with lips parted graciously over teeth as white as milk; colour the skin with the down of a peach that no hand has touched, and you will have the general aspect of that charming countenance. The hair, black as jet, waving naturally or not, was parted on the forehead in two large folds and draped back over the head, leaving in sight just the tip of the ears, in which there glittered two diamonds, worth four to five thousand francs each. How it was that her ardent life had left on Marguerite's face the virginal, almost childlike expression which characterized it, is a problem which we can but state, without attempting to solve it.

Marguerite had a marvellous portrait of herself, by Vidal, the only man whose pencil could do her justice. I had this portrait by me for a few days after her death, and the likeness was so astonishing that it has helped to refresh my memory in regard to some points which I might not otherwise have remembered.

Some among the details of this chapter did not reach me until later, but I write them here so as not to be obliged to return to them when the story itself has begun.

Marguerite was always present at every first night, and passed every evening either at the theatre or the ball. Whenever there was a new piece she was certain to be seen, and she invariably had three things with her on the ledge of her ground-floor box: her opera-glass, a bag of sweets, and a bouquet of camellias.

For twenty-five days of the month the camellias were white, and for five they were red; no one ever knew the reason of this change of colour, which I mention though I can not explain it; it was noticed both by her friends and by the *habitués* of the theatres to which she most often went. She was never seen with any flowers but camellias. At the florist's, Madame Barjon's, she had come to be called 'the Lady of the Camellias', and the name stuck to her.

Like all those who move in a certain set in Paris, I knew that Marguerite had lived with some of the most fashionable young men in society, that she spoke of it openly, and that they themselves boasted of it; so that all seemed equally pleased with one another. Nevertheless, for about three years, after a visit to Bagnères, she was said to be living with an old duke, a foreigner, enormously rich, who had tried to remove her as far as possible from her former life, and, as it seemed, entirely to her own satisfaction.

This is what I was told on the subject. In the spring of 1842 Marguerite was so ill that the doctors ordered her to take the waters, and she went to Bagnères. Among the invalids was the daughter of this duke; she was not only suffering from the same complaint, but she was so like Marguerite in appearance that they might have been taken for sisters; the young duchess was in the last stage of consumption, and a few days after Marguerite's arrival she died.

One morning, the duke, who had remained at Bagnères to be near the soil that had buried a part of his heart, caught sight of Marguerite at a turn of the road. He seemed to see the shadow of his child, and going up to her, he took her hands, embraced and wept over her, and without even asking her who she was, begged her to let him love in her the living image of his dead child. Marguerite, alone at Bagnères with her maid, and not being in any fear of compromising herself, granted the duke's request. Some people who knew her, happening to be at Bagnères, took upon themselves to explain Mademoiselle Gautier's true postion to the duke. It was a blow to the old man, for the resemblance with his daughter ended in one direction, but it was too late. She had become a necessity to his heart, his only pretext, his only excuse, for living. He made no reproaches, he had indeed no right to do so, but he asked her if she felt herself capable of changing her mode of life, offering her in return for the sacrifice every compensation that she could desire. She consented.

It must be said that Marguerite was just then very ill. The past seemed to her sensitive nature as if it were one of the main causes of her illness, and a sort of superstition led her to hope that God would restore to her both health and beauty in return for her repentance and conversion. By the end of the summer, the waters, sleep, the natural fatigue of long walks, had indeed more or less restored her health. The duke accompanied her to Paris, where he continued to see her as he had done at Bagnères.

This liaison, whose motive and origin were quite unknown, caused a great sensation, for the duke, already known for his immense fortune, now became known for his prodigality. All this was set down to the debauchery of a rich old man, and everything was believed except the truth. The father's sentiment for Marguerite had, in truth, so pure a cause that anything but a communion of hearts would have seemed to him a kind of incest, and he had never spoken to her a word which his daughter might not have heard.

Far be it from me to make out our heroine to be anything but what she was. As long as she remained at Bagnères, the promise she had made to the duke had not been hard to keep, and she had kept it; but, once back in Paris, it seemed to her – accustomed to a life of dissipation, of balls, of orgies – as if the solitude, only interrupted by the duke's stated visits, would kill her with boredom, and the hot breath of her old life came back across her head and heart.

We must add that Marguerite had returned more beautiful than she had ever been; she was about twenty, and her malady, sleeping but not subdued, continued to give her those feverish desires which are almost always the result of diseases of the chest.

It was a great grief to the duke when his friends, always on the lookout for some scandal on the part of the woman with whom, it seemed to them, he was compromising himself, came to tell him, indeed, to prove to him, that at times when she was sure of not seeing him she received other visits, and that these visits were often prolonged till the following day. On being questioned, Marguerite admitted everything to the duke, and advised him, without *arrière-pensée*, to concern himself with her no longer, for she felt incapable of carrying out what she had undertaken, and she did not wish to go on accepting benefits from a man whom she was deceiving. The duke did not return for a week; it was all he could do, and on the eighth day he came to beg Marguerite to let him still visit her, promising that he would take her as she was, so long as he might see her, and swearing that he would never utter a reproach against her, not though he were to die of it.

This, then, was the state of things three months after Marguerite's return; that is to say, in November or December, 1842.

CHAPTER III

At one o'clock on the 16th I went to the Rue d'Antin. The voice of the auctioneer could be heard from the outer door. The rooms were crowded with people. There were all the celebrities of the most elegant impropriety, furtively examined by certain great ladies who had again seized the opportunity of the sale in order to be able to see, close at hand, women whom they might never have another occasion of meeting, and whom they envied perhaps in secret for their easy pleasures. The Duchess of F. elbowed Mlle. A., one of the most melancholy examples of our modern courtesan. The Marquis de T. hesitated over a piece of furniture the price of which was being run high by Mme. D., the most elegant and famous adulteress of our time. The Duke of Y., who in Madrid is supposed to be ruining himself in Paris, and in Paris to be ruining himself in Madrid, and who, as a matter of fact, never even reaches the limit of his income, talked with Mme. M., one of our wittiest story-tellers, who from time to time writes what she says and signs what she writes. At the same time he exchanged confidential glances with Mme. de N., a fair ornament of the Champs-Élysées, almost always dressed in pink or blue, and driving two big black horses which Tony had sold her for 10,000 francs, and for which she had paid, after her fashion. finally, Mlle. R., who makes by her mere talent twice what the women of the world make by their dowry and three times as much as the others make by their amours, had come, in spite of the cold, to make some purchases, and was not the least looked at among the crowd.

I might cite the initials of many more of those who found themselves, not without some mutual surprise, side by side in one room. But I fear to weary the reader. I will only add that every one was in the highest spirits, and that many of those present had known the dead woman, and seemed quite oblivious of the fact. There was the sound of loud laughter.

The auctioneers shouted at the top of their voices. The dealers who had filled the benches in front of the auction table tried in vain to obtain silence, in order to transact their business in peace. Never was there a noisier or a more varied gathering.

I slipped quietly into the midst of this tumult, sad to think that the poor creature whose goods were being sold to pay her debts had died in the next room. Having come rather to examine than to buy, I watched the faces of the auctioneers, noticing how they beamed with delight whenever anything reached a price beyond their expectations. Honest creatures, who had speculated upon this woman's prostitution, who had gained their hundred per cent out of her, who had plagued their claims the last moments of her life, and who came now after her death to gather in, at once, the fruits of their dishonourable calculations and the interest on their shameful credit! How wise were the ancients in having only one God for traders and robbers!

Dresses, cashmeres, jewels, were sold with incredible rapidity. There was nothing that I cared for, and I still waited. All at once I heard: 'A volume, beautifully bound, gilt-edged, entitled Manon Lescaut. There is something written on the first page. Ten francs.'

'Twelve,' said a voice after a longish silence.

'Fifteen,' I said.

Why? I did not know. Doubtless for the something written.

'Fifteen,' repeated the auctioneer.

'Thirty,' said the first bidder in a tone which seemed to defy further competition.

It had now become a struggle. 'Thirty-five,' I cried in the same tone.

'Forty.'

'Fifty.'

'Sixty.'

'A hundred.'

If I had wished to make a sensation I should certainly have succeeded, for a profound silence had ensued, and people gazed at me as if to see what sort of a person it was who seemed to be so determined to possess the volume.

The accent which I had given to my last word seemed to convince my adversary; he preferred to abandon a conflict which could only have resulted in making me pay ten times its price for the volume, and, bowing, he said very gracefully, though indeed a little late:

'I give way, sir.'

Nothing more being offered, the book was assigned to me.

As I was afraid of some new fit of obstinacy, which my *amour propre* might have sustained somewhat better than my purse, I wrote down my name, had the book put on one side, and went out. I must have given considerable food for reflection to the witnesses of this scene, who would no doubt ask themselves what my purpose could have been in paying a hundred francs for a book, which I could have had anywhere for ten, or, at the outside, fifteen.

An hour after, I sent for my purchase. On the first page was written in ink, in an elegant hand, an inscription on the part of the giver. It consisted of these words:

> *Manon to Marguerite.*
> *Humility.*

It was signed Armand Duval.

What was the meaning of the word Humility? Was Manon to recognize in Marguerite, in the opinion of M. Armand Duval, her superior in vice or in affection? The second interpretation seemed the more probable for the first would have been an impertinent piece of plain speaking which Marguerite, whatever her opinion of herself, would never have accepted.

I went out again, and thought no more of the book until at night, when I was going to bed.

Manon Lescaut is a touching story. I know every detail of it, and yet whenever I come across the volume the same sympathy always draws me to it. I open it, and for the hundredth time I live over again with the heroine of the Abbé Prévost. Now, this heroine is so true to life that I feel as if I had known her. The sort of comparison between her and Marguerite gave me an unusual inclination to read it, and my indulgence passed into pity, almost into a kind of love for the poor girl to whom I owed the volume. Manon died in the desert, it is true, but in the arms of the man who loved her with the whole energy of his soul; who, when she was dead, dug a grave for her, and watered it with his tears, and buried his heart in it; while Marguerite, a sinner like Manon, and perhaps converted like her, had died in a sumptuous bed (it seemed, after what I had seen, the bed of her past), but in that desert of the heart, a more barren, a vaster, a more pitiless desert than that in which Manon had found her last resting-place.

Marguerite, in fact, as I had found from some friends who knew of the last cicumstances of her life, had not a single real friend by her bedside, during the two months of her long and painful agony.

Then from Manon and Margeurite my mind wandered to those whom I knew, and whom I saw singing along the way which led to just such another death. Poor souls! if it is not right to love them, is-it not well to pity them? You pity the blind man who has never seen the daylight, the deaf who has never heard the harmonies of nature, the dumb who has never found a voice for his soul. Yet, under a false cloak of shame, you will not pity this blindness of heart, this deafness of soul, this dumbness of conscience, which sets the poor afflicted creature beside herself and makes her, in spite of herself, incapable of seeing what is good, of hearing the Lord, and of speaking the pure language of love and faith.

Hugo has written Marion Delorme, Musset has written Bernerette, Alexandre Dumas has written Fernande, the thinkers and poets of all time have brought to the courtesan the offering of their pity, and at times a great man has rehabilitated them with his love and even with his name. If I insist on this point, it is because many readers might be ready to throw down a book in which they will fear to find an apology for vice and prostitution; and the author's youth will do something, no doubt, to increase this fear. Let me undeceive those who think thus, and let them go on reading, if nothing but such a fear hinders them.

I am quite simply convinced of a certain principle, which is: For the woman whose education has not taught her what is right, God almost always opens two ways which lead there, the ways of sorrow and love. They are hard; those who walk in them walk with bleeding feet and torn hands, but they also leave the trappings of vice upon the thorns of the wayside, and reach the journey's end in a nakedness which is not shameful in the sight of the Lord.

Those who meet these bold travellers ought to succour them, and to tell all that they have met them, for in so doing they point out the way. It is not a question of setting at the outset of life two sign-posts, one bearing the inscription 'The Right Way', the other the inscription 'The Wrong Way', and of saying to those who come there, 'Choose'. One must needs, like Christ, point out the ways which lead from the second road to the first, to those who have been easily led astray; and it is needful that the beginning of these ways should not be too painful nor appear too impenetrable.

Here is Christianity with its marvellous parable of the Prodigal Son to teach us indulgence and pardon. Jesus was full of love for souls wounded by the passions of men; he loved to bind up their wounds and to find in those very wounds the balm which should heal them. Thus he said to the Magdalen: 'Much shall be forgiven thee because thou hast loved much,' a sublimity of pardon which can only have called forth a sublime faith.

Why do we make ourselves more strict than Christ? Why, holding obstinately to the opinions of the world, which hardens itself in order that it may be thought strong, do we reject as it rejects, souls bleeding at wounds by which, like a sick man's bad blood, the evil of their past may be healed, if only a friendly hand is stretched out to lave them and set them in the convalescence of the heart?

It is to my own generation that I speak, to those for whom the theories of M. de Voltaire happily exist no longer, to those who, like myself, realize that humanity, in these last years, has been in one of its most audacious moments of expansion. The science of good and evil is acquired forever; faith is refashioned, respect for sacred things has returned to us, and if the world has not all at once become good, it has at least become better. The efforts of every intelligent man tend in the same direction, and every strong will is harnessed to the same principle: Be good, be young, be true! Evil is nothing but vanity, let us have the pride of good, and above all let us never despair. Do not let us despise the woman who is neither mother, sister, maid, nor wife. Do not let us limit esteem to the family nor indulgence to egoism. Since 'there is more joy in heaven over one sinner that repenteth than over ninety and nine just persons that need no repentance', let us give joy to heaven. Heaven will render it back to us with usury. Let us leave on our way the alms of pardon for those whom earthly desires have driven astray, whom a divine hope shall perhaps save, and, as old women say when they offer you some homely remedy of their own, if it does no good it will do no harm.

Doubtless it must seem a bold thing to attempt to deduce these grand results out of the meagre subject that I deal with; but I am one of those who believe that all is in little. The child is small, and he includes the man; the brain is narrow, and it harbours thought; the eye is but a point, and it covers miles.

CHAPTER IV

Two days after, the sale was ended. It had produced 150,000 francs. The creditors divided among them two-thirds, and the family, a sister and a grand-nephew, received the remainder.

The sister opened her eyes very wide when the lawyer wrote to her that she had inherited 50,000 francs. The girl had not seen her sister for six or seven years, and did not know what had become of her from the moment when she had disappeared from home. She came to Paris in haste, and great was the astonishment of those who had known Marguerite when they saw as her only heir a fine fat country girl, who until then had never left her village. She had made the fortune at a single stroke, without even knowing the source of that fortune. She went back, I heard afterward, to her countryside, greatly saddened by her sister's death, but with a sadness which was somewhat lightened by the investment at four and a half per cent which she had been able to make.

All these circumstances, often repeated in Paris, the mother city of scandal, had begun to be forgotten, and I was even little by little forgetting the part I had taken in them, when a new incident brought to my knowledge the whole of Marguerite's life, and acquainted me with such pathetic details that I was taken with the idea of writing down the story which I now write.

The rooms, now emptied of all their furniture, had been to let for three or four days when one morning there was a ring at my door.

My servant, or, rather, my porter, who acted as my servant, went to the door and brought me a card, saying that the person who had given it to him wished to see me.

I glanced at the card and there read these two words: *Armand Duval.*

I tried to think where I had seen the name, and remembered the first leaf of the copy of Manon Lescaut. What could the

17

person who had given the book to Marguerite want of me? I gave orders to ask him in at once.

I saw a young man, blond, tall, pale, dressed in a travelling suit which looked as if he had not changed it for some days, and had not even taken the trouble to brush it on arriving at Paris, for it was covered with dust.

M. Duval was deeply agitated; he made no attempt to conceal his agitation, and it was with tears in his eyes and a trembling voice that he said to me:

'Sir, I beg you to excuse my visit and my costume; but young people are not very ceremonious with one another, and I was so anxious to see you today that I have not even gone to the hotel to which I have sent my luggage, and have rushed straight here, fearing that, after all, I might miss you, early as it is.'

I begged M. Duval to sit down by the fire; he did so, and, taking his handkerchief from his pocket, hid his face in it for a moment.

'You must be at a loss to understand,' he went on, sighing sadly, 'for what purpose an unknown visitor, at such an hour, in such a costume, can have come to see you. I have simply come to ask of you a great service.'

'Speak on, sir, I am entirely at your disposal.'

'You were present at the sale of Marguerite Gautier?'

At this word the emotion, which he had got the better of for an instant, was too much for him, and he was obliged to cover his eyes with his hand.

'I must seem to you very absurd,' he added, 'but pardon me, and believe that I shall never forget the patience with which you have listened to me'.

'Sir,' I answered, 'if the service which I can render you is able to lessen your trouble a little, tell me at once what I can do for you, and you will find me only too happy to oblige you.'

M. Duval's sorrow was sympathetic, and in spite of myself I felt the desire of doing him a kindness. Thereupon he said to me:

'You bought something at Marguerite's sale?'

'Yes, a book.'

'Manon Lescaut?'

'Precisely.'

'Have you the book still?'

'It is in my bedroom.'

On hearing this, Armand Duval seemed to be relieved of a great weight, and thanked me as if I had already rendered him a service merely by keeping the book.

I got up and went into my room to fetch the book, which I handed to him.

'That is it indeed,' he said, looking at the inscription on the first page and turning over the leaves; 'that is it indeed,' and two big tears fell on the pages. 'Well, sir,' said he, lifting his head, and no longer trying to hide from me that he had wept and was even then on the point of weeping, 'do you value this book very greatly?'

'Why?'

'Because I have come to ask you to give it up to me.'

'Pardon my curiosity, but was it you, then, who gave it to Marguerite Gautier?'

'It was I.'

'The book is yours, sir; take it back. I am happy to be able to hand it over to you.'

'But,' said M. Duval with some embarrassment, 'the least I can do is to give you in return the price which you paid for it.'

'Allow me to offer it to you. The price of a single volume in a sale of that kind is a mere nothing, and I do not remember how much I gave for it.'

'You gave one hundred francs.'

'True,' I said, embarrassed in my turn, 'how do you know?'

'It is quite simple. I hoped to reach Paris in time for the sale, and I only managed to get here this morning. I was absolutely resolved to have something which had belonged to her, and I hastened to the auctioneer and asked him to allow me to see the list of the things sold and of the buyers' names. I saw that this volume had been bought by you, and I decided to ask you to give it up to me, though the price you had set upon it made me fear that you might yourself have some souvenir in connection with the possession of the book.'

As he spoke, it was evident that he was afraid I had known Marguerite as he had known her, I hastened to reassure him.

'I knew Mlle. Gautier only by sight,' I said; 'her death made on me the impression that the death of a pretty woman must always make on a young man who had liked seeing her. I wished to buy something at her sale, and I bid higher and higher for this book out of mere obstinacy and to annoy some one else, who was equally keen to obtain it, and who seemed to defy me to the contest. I repeat, then, that the book is yours, and once more I beg you to accept it; do not treat me as if I were an auctioneer, and let it be the pledge between us of a longer and more intimate acquaintance.'

'Good,' said Armand, holding out his hand and pressing mine; 'I accept, and I shall be grateful to you all my life.'

I was very anxious to question Armand on the subject of Marguerite, for the inscription in the book, the young man's hurried journey, his desire to possess the volume, piqued my curiosity; but I feared if I questioned my visitor that I might seem to have refused his money only in order to have the right to pry into his affairs.

It was as if he guessed my desire, for he said to me:

'Have you read the volume?'

'All through.'

'What did you think of the two lines that I wrote in it?'

'I realized at once that the woman to whom you had given the volume must have been quite outside the ordinary category, for I could not take those two lines as a mere empty compliment.'

'You were right. That woman was an angel. See, read this letter.' And he handed to me a paper which seemed to have been many times reread.

I opened it, and this is what it contained:

'MY DEAR ARMAND: I have received your letter. You are still good, and I thank God for it. Yes, my friend, I am ill, and with one of those diseases that never relent; but the interest you still take in me makes my suffering less. I shall not live long enough, I expect, to have the happiness of pressing the hand which has written the kind letter I have just received; the words of it would be enough to cure me. I shall not see you, for I am quite near death, and you are hundreds of miles away. My poor friend! your Marguerite of old times is sadly changed. It is better perhaps for you not to see her again than to see her as she is. You ask if I forgive you; oh, with all my heart, friend, for the way you hurt me was only a way of proving the love you had for me. I have been in bed for a month, and I think so much of your esteem that I write every day the journal of my life, from the moment we left each other to the moment when I shall be able to write no longer. If the interest you take in me is real, Armand, when you come back go and see Julie Duprat. She will give you my journal. You will find in it the reason and the excuse for what has passed between us. Julie is very good to me; we often talk of you together. She was there when your letter came, and we both cried over it.

'If you had not sent me any word, I would have told her to give you those papers when you returned to France. Do not thank me for it. This daily looking back on the only happy moments of my life does me an immense amount of good, and if you will find in reading it some excuse for the past, I, for my part, find a continual solace in it. I should like to leave you something which would always remind you of me, but everything here has been seized, and I have nothing of my own.

'Do you understand my friend? I am dying, and from my bed I can hear a man walking to and fro in the drawing room; my creditors have put him there to see that nothing is taken away, and that nothing remains to me in case I do not die. I hope they will wait till the end before they begin to sell.

'Oh, men have no pity! or rather, I am wrong, it is God who is just and inflexible!

'And now, dear love, you will come to my sale, and you will buy something, for if I put aside the least thing for you, they might accuse you of embezzling seized goods.

'It is a sad life that I am leaving!

'It would be good of God to let me see you again before I die. According to all probability, good-bye, my friend. Pardon me if I do not write a longer letter, but those who say they are going to cure me wear me out with blood-letting, and my hand refuses to write anymore.

'MARGUERITE GAUTIER.'

The last two words were scarcely legible. I returned the letter to Armand, who had, no doubt, read it over again in his mind while I was reading it on paper, for he said to me as he took it:

'Who would think that a kept woman could have written that?' And, overcome by recollections, he gazed for some time at the writing of the letter, which he finally carried to his lips.

'And when I think,' he went on, 'that she died before I could see her, and that I shall never see her again, when I think that she did for me what no sister would ever have done, I cannot forgive myself for having left her to die like that. Dead! Dead and thinking of me, writing and repeating my name, poor dead Marguerite!'

And Armand, giving free outlet to his thoughts and his tears, held out his hand to me, and continued:

'People would think it childish enough if they saw me lament like this over a dead woman such as she; no one will ever know what I made that woman suffer, how cruel I have been to her! how good, how resigned she was! I thought it was I who had to forgive her, and today I feel unworthy of the forgiveness which she grants me. Oh, I would give ten years of my life to weep at her feet for an hour!'

It is always difficult to console a sorrow that is unknown to one, and nevertheless I felt so lively a sympathy for the young man, he made me so frankly the confidant of his distress, that I believed a word from me would not be indifferent to him, and I said:

'Have you no parents, no friends? Hope. Go and see them; they will console you. As for me, I can only pity you.'

'It is true,' he said, rising and walking to and fro in the room, 'I am wearying you. Pardon me, I did not reflect how little my sorrow must mean to you, and that I am intruding upon you something which can not and ought not to interest you at all.'

'You mistake my meaning. I am entirely at your service; only I regret my inability to calm your distress. If my society and that of my friends can give you any distraction, if, in short, you have need of me, no matter in what way, I hope you will realize how much pleasure it will give me to do anything for you.'

'Pardon, pardon,' said he; 'sorrow sharpens the sensations. Let me stay here for a few minutes longer, long enough to dry

my eyes, so that the idlers in the street may not look upon it as
a curiosity to see a big fellow like me crying. You have made
my very happy by giving me this book. I do not know how I
can ever express my gratitude to you.'

'By giving me a little of your friendship,' said I, 'and by
telling me the cause of your suffering. One feels better while
telling what one suffers.'

'You are right. But today I have too much need of tears; I
can not very well talk. One day I will tell you the whole story,
and you will see if I have reason for regretting the poor girl.
And now,' he added, rubbing his eyes for the last time, and
looking at himself in the glass, 'say that you do not think me
too absolutely idiotic, and allow me to come back and see you
another time.'

He cast on me a gentle and amiable look. I was near
embracing him. As for him, his eyes again began to fill with
tears; he saw that I perceived it and turned away his head.

'Come,' I said, 'courage.'

'Good-bye,' he said.

And, making a desperate effort to restrain his tears, he
rushed rather than went out of the room.

I lifted the curtain of my window, and saw him get into the
cabriolet which awaited him at the door; but scarcely was he
seated before he burst into tears and hid his face in his pocket
handkerchief.

CHAPTER V

A good while elapsed before I heard anything more of Armand, but, on the other hand, I was constantly hearing of Marguerite.

I do not know if you have noticed, if once the name of anybody who might in the natural course of things have always remained unknown, or at all events indifferent to you, should be mentioned before you, immediately details begin to group themselves about the name, and you will find all your friends talking to you about something which they have never mentioned to you before. You discover that this person was almost touching you and has passed close to you many times in your life without your noticing it; you find coincidences in the events which are told you, a real affinity with certain events of your own existence. I was not absolutely at that point in regard to Marguerite, for I had seen and met her, I knew her by sight and by reputation. Nevertheless, since the moment of the sale, her name came to my ears so frequently, and, owing to the circumstance that I have mentioned in the last chapter, that name was associated with so profound a sorrow, that my curiosity increased in proportion with my astonishment. The consequence was that whenever I met friends to whom I had never breathed the name of Marguerite, I always began by saying:

'Did you ever know a certain Marguerite Gautier?'

'The Lady of the Camellias?'

'Exactly.'

'Oh, very well!'

The word was sometimes accompanied by a smile which could leave no doubt as to its meaning.

'Well, what sort of a girl was she?'

'A good sort of girl.'

'Is that all?'

'Oh, yes; more intelligence and perhaps a little more heart than most.'

'Do you know anything particular about her?'

'She ruined Baron de G.'

'No more than that?'

'She was the mistress of the old Duke of . . .'

'Was she really his mistress?'

'So they say; at all events, he gave her a great deal of his money.'

The general outlines were always the same. Nevertheless I was anxious to find out something about the relations between Marguerite and Armand. Meeting one day a man who was constantly about with known women, I asked him: 'Did you know Marguerite Gautier?'

The answer was the usual 'Very well.'

'What sort of a girl was she?'

'A fine, good girl. I was very sorry to hear of her death.'

'Had she not a lover called Armand Duval?'

'Tall and blond?'

'Yes.'

'It is quite true.'

'Who was this Armand?'

'A fellow who squandered on her the little money he had, and then had to leave her. They say he was quite wild about it.'

'And she?'

'They always say she was very much in love with him, but as girls like that are in love. It is no good to ask them for what they can not give.'

'What became of Armand?'

'I don't know. We knew him very little. He was with Marguerite for five or six months in the country. When she came back, he had gone.'

'And you have never seen him since?'

'Never.'

I, too, had not seen Armand again. I was beginning to ask myself if, when he had come to see me, the recent news of Marguerite's death had not exaggerated his former love, and consequently his sorrow, and I said to myself that perhaps he had already forgotten the dead woman, and along with her his promise to come and see me again. This supposition would have seemed probable enough in most instances, but in

Armand's despair there had been an accent of real sincerity, and, going from one extreme to another, I imagined that distress had brought on an illness, and that my not seeing him was explained by the fact that he was ill, perhaps dead.

I was interested in the young man in spite of myself. Perhaps there was some selfishness in this interest; perhaps I guessed at some pathetic love story under all this sorrow; perhaps my desire to know all about it had much to do with the anxiety which Armand's silence had caused me.

Since M. Duval did not return to me, I decided to go and see him. A pretext was not difficult to find; unluckily I did not know his address, and no one among those whom I questioned could give it to me.

I went to the Rue d'Antin; perhaps Marguerite's porter would know where Armand lived. There was a new porter; he knew as little about it as I. I then asked in which cemetery Mlle. Gautier had been buried. It was the Montmartre Cemetery. It was now the month of April; the weather was fine, the graves were not likely to look as sad and desolate as they do in winter; in short it was warm enough for the living to think a little of the dead, and pay them a visit. I went to the cemetery, saying to myself: 'One glance at Marguerite's grave, and I shall know if Armand's sorrow still exists, and perhaps I may find out what has become of him.'

I entered the keeper's lodge, and asked him if on the 22nd of February a woman named Marguerite Gautier had not been buried in the Montmartre Cemetery. He turned over the pages of a big book in which those who enter this last resting-place are inscribed and numbered, and replied that on the 22nd of February, at 12 o'clock, a woman of that name had been buried.

I asked him to show me the grave, for there is no finding one's way without a guide in this city of the dead, which has its streets like a city of the living. The keeper called over a gardener, to whom he gave the necessary instructions; the gardener interrupted him, saying: 'I know, I know. – It is not difficult to find that grave,' he added, turning to me.

'Why?'

'Because it has very different flowers from the others.'

'Is it you who look after it?'

'Yes, sir; and I wish all relations took as much trouble about the dead as the young man who gave me my orders.'

After several turnings, the gardener stopped and said to me: 'Here we are.'

I saw before me a square of flowers which one would never have taken for a grave, if it had not been for a white marble slab bearing a name.

The marble slab stood upright, an iron railing marked the limits of the ground purchased, and the earth was covered with white camellias.

'What do you say to that?' said the gardener.

'It is beautiful.'

'And whenever a camellia fades, I have orders to replace it.'

'Who gave you the order?'

'A young gentleman who cried the first time he came here; an old pal of hers, I suppose, for they say she was a gay one. Very pretty, too, I believe. Did you know her, sir?'

'Yes.'

'Like the other?' said the gardener, with a knowing smile.

'No, I never spoke to her.'

'And you come here, too! It is very good of you, for those that come to see the poor girl don't exactly cumber the cemetery.'

'Doesn't anybody come?'

'Nobody, except that young gentleman who came once.'

'Only once?'

'Yes, sir.'

'He never came back again?'

'No, but he will when he gets home.'

'He is away somewhere?'

'Yes.'

'Do you know where he is?'

'I believe he has gone to see Mlle. Gautier's sister.'

'What does he want there?'

'He has gone to get her authority to have the corpse dug up again and put somewhere else.'

'Why won't he let it remain here?'

'You know, sir, people have queer notions about dead folk. We see something of that every day. The ground here was only bought for five years, and this young gentleman wants a perpetual lease and a bigger plot of ground; it will be better in the new part.'

'What do you call the new part?'

'The new plots of ground that are for sale, there to the left. If the cemetery had always been kept like it is now, there wouldn't be the like of it in the world; but there is still plenty to do before it will be quite all it should be. And then people are so queer!'

'What do you mean?'

'I mean that there are people who carry their pride even here. Now, this Demoiselle Gautier, it appears she lived a bit free, if you'll excuse me saying so. Poor lady, she's dead now; there's no more of her left than of them that no one has a word to say against. We water them every day. Well, when the relatives of the folk that are buried beside her found out the sort of person she was, what do you think they said? That they would try to keep her out from here, and that there ought to be a piece of ground somewhere apart for this sort of woman, like there is for the poor. Did you ever hear of such a thing? I gave it to them straight, I did: well-to-do folk who come to see their dead four times a year, and bring their flowers themselves, and what flowers! and look twice at the keep of them they pretend to cry over, and write on their tombstones all about the tears they haven't shed, and come and make difficulties about their neighbours. You may believe me or not, sir, I never knew the young lady; I don't know what she did. Well, I'm quite in love with the poor thing; I look after her well, and I let her have her camellias at an honest price. She is the dead body that I like the best. You see, sir, we are obliged to love the dead, for we are kept so busy, we have hardly time to love anything else.'

I looked at the man, and some of my readers will understand, without my needing to explain it to them, the emotion which I felt on hearing him. He observed it, no doubt, for he went on:

'They tell me there were people who ruined themselves over that girl, and lovers that worshipped her; well, when I think there isn't one of them that so much as buys her a flower now, that's queer, sir, and sad. And, after all, she isn't so badly off, for she has her grave to herself, and if there is only one who remembers her, he makes up for the others. But we have other poor girls here, just like her and just her age, and they are just thrown into a pauper's grave, and it breaks my heart when I hear their poor bodies drop into the earth. And not a soul thinks about them any more, once they are dead! 'Tisn't a merry trade, ours, especially when we have a little heart left. What do you expect? I can't help it. I have a fine, strapping girl myself; she's just twenty, and when a girl of that age comes here I think of her, and I don't care if it's a great lady or a vagabond, I can't help feeling it a bit. But I am taking up your time, sir, with my tales, and it wasn't to hear them you came here. I was told to show you Mlle. Gautier's grave; here you have it. Is there anything else I can do for you?'

'Do you know M. Armand Duval's address?' I asked.

'Yes; he lives at Rue de ——; at least, that's where I always go to get my money for the flowers you see there.'

'Thanks, my good man.'

I gave one more look at the grave covered with flowers half longing to penetrate the depths of the earth and see what the earth had made of the fair creature that had been cast to it; then I walked sadly away.

'Do you want to see M. Duval, sir?' said the gardener, who was walking beside me.

'Yes.'

'Well, I am pretty sure he is not back yet, or he would have been here already.'

'You don't think he has forgotten Marguerite?'

'I am not only sure he hasn't, but I would wager that he wants to change her grave simply in order to have one more look at her.'

'Why do you think that?'

'The first word he said to me when he came to the cemetery was:"How can I see her again?" That can't be done unless there is a change of grave, and I told him all about the formalities that have to be attended to in getting it done; for, you see, if you want to move a body from one grave to another you must have it identified, and only the family can give leave for it under the direction of a police inspector. That is why M. Duval has gone to see Mlle. Gautier's sister, and you may be sure his first visit will be to me.'

We had come to the cemetery gate. I thanked the gardener again, putting a few coins into his hand, and made my way to the address he had given me.

Armand had not yet returned. I left word for him, begging him to come and see me as soon as he arrived, or to send me word where I could find him.

Next day, in the morning, I received a letter from Duval, telling me of his return, and asking me to call on him, as he was so worn out with fatigue that it was impossible for him to go out.

CHAPTER VI

I found Armand in bed. On seeing me he held out a burning hand.

'You are feverish,' I said to him.

'It is nothing, the fatigue of a rapid journey; that is all.'

'You have been to see Marguerite's sister?'

'Yes; who told you?'

'I know it. Did you get what you wanted?'

'Yes; but who told you of my journey, and of my reason for taking it?'

'The gardener of the cemetery.'

'You have seen the tomb?'

I scarcely dared reply, for the tone in which the words were spoken proved to me that the speaker was still possessed by the emotion which I had witnessed before, and that every time his thoughts or speech travelled back to that mournful subject emotion would still, for a long time to come, prove stronger than his will. I contented myself with a nod of the head.

'He has looked after it well?' continued Armand. Two big tears rolled down the cheeks of the sick man, and he turned away his head to hide them from me. I pretended not to see them, and tried to change the conversation.

'You have been away three weeks,' I said.

Armand passed his hand across his eyes and replied, 'Exactly three weeks.'

'You had a long journey.'

'Oh, I was not travelling all the time. I was ill for a fortnight, or I should have returned long ago; but I had scarcely got there when I took this fever, and I was obliged to keep my room.'

'And you started to come back before you were really well?'

'If I had remained in the place for another week, I should have died there.'

31

'Well, you are back again, you must take care of yourself; your friends will come and look after you; myself, first of all, if you will allow me.'

'I shall get up in a couple of hours.'

'It would be very unwise.'

'I must.'

'What have you to do in such a great hurry?'

'I must go to the inspector of police.'

'Why do you not get one of your friends to see after the matter? It is likely to make you worse than you are now.'

'It is my only chance of getting better. I must see her. Ever since I heard of her death, expecially since I saw her grave, I have not been able to sleep. I can not realize that this woman, so young and so beautiful when I left her, is really dead. I must convince myself of it. I must see what God has done with a being that I have loved so much, and perhaps the horror of the sight will cure me of my despair. Will you accompany me, if it won't be troubling you too much?'

'What did her sister say about it?'

'Nothing. She seemed greatly surprised that a stranger wanted to buy a plot of ground and give Marguerite a new grave, and she immediately signed the authorization that I asked her for.'

'Believe me, it would be better to wait until you are quite well.'

'Have no fear; I shall be quite composed. Besides, I should simply go out of my mind if I were not to carry out a resolution which I have set myself to carry out. I swear to you that I shall never be myself again until I have seen Marguerite. It is perhaps the thirst of the fever, a sleepless night's dream, a moment's delirium; but though I were to become a Trappist, like M. de Rancé, after having seen, I will see.'

'I understand,' I said to Armand, 'and I am at your service. Have you seen Julie Duprat?'

'Yes, I saw her the day I returned, for the first time.'

'Did she give you the papers that Marguerite had left for you?'

Armand drew a roll of papers from under his pillow, and immediately put them back.

'I know all that is in these papers by heart,' he said. 'For three weeks I have read them ten times over every day. You shall read them, too, but later on, when I am calmer, and can make you understand all the love and tenderness hidden away in this confession. For the moment I want you to do me a service.'

'What is it?'

'Your cab is below?'

'Yes.'

'Well, will you take my passport and ask if there are any letters for me at the post office? My father and sister must have written to me at Paris, and I went away in such a haste that I did not go and see before leaving. When you come back we will go together to the inspector of police, and arrange for tomorrow's ceremony.'

Armand handed me his passport, and I went to Rue Jean Jacques Rousseau. There were two letters addressed to Duval. I took them and returned. When I re-entered the room Armand was dressed and ready to go out.

'Thanks,' he said, taking out the letters. 'Yes,' he added, after glancing at the addresses, 'they are from my father and sister. They must have been quite at a loss to understand my silence.'

He opened the letters, guessed at rather than read them, for each was of four pages; and a moment after folded them up. 'Come,' he said, 'I will answer tomorrow.'

We went to the police station, and Armand handed in the permission signed by Marguerite's sister. He received in return a letter to the keeper of the cemetery, and it was settled that the disinterment was to take place next day, at ten o'clock, that I should call for him an hour before, and that we should go to the cemetery together.

I confess that I was curious to be present, and I did not sleep all night. Judging from the thoughts which filled my brain, it must have been a long night for Armand. When I entered his room at nine on the following morning he was frightfully pale, but seemed calm. He smiled and held out his hand. His candles were burned out; and before leaving he took a very heavy letter addressed to his father, and no doubt containing an account of that night's impressions.

Half an hour later we were at Montmartre. The police inspector was there already. We walked slowly in the direction of Marguerite's grave. The inspector went in front; Armand and I followed a few steps behind.

From time to time I felt my companion's arm tremble convulsively, as if he shivered from head to feet. I looked at him. He understood the look, and smiled at me; we had not exchanged a word since leaving the house.

Just before we reached the grave, Armand stopped to wipe his face, which was covered with great drops of sweat. I took advantage of the pause to draw in a long breath, for I, too, felt as if I had a weight on my chest.

What is the origin of that mournful pleasure which we find in sights of this kind? When we reached the grave the gardener had removed all the flower-pots, the iron railing had been taken away, and two men were turning up the soil.

Armand leaned against a tree and watched. All his life seemed to pass before his eyes. Suddenly one of the two pickaxes struck against a stone. At the sound Armand recoiled, as at an electric shock, and seized my hand with such force as to give me pain.

One of the grave-diggers took a shovel and began emptying out the earth; then, when only the stones covering the coffin were left, he threw them out one by one.

I scrutinized Armand, for every moment I was afraid lest the emotions which he was visibly repressing should prove too much for him; but he still watched, his eyes fixed and wide open, like the eyes of a madman, and a slight trembling of the cheeks and lips were the only signs of the violent nervous crisis under which he was suffering.

As for me, all I can say is that I regretted having come.

When the coffin was uncovered the inspector said to the grave-digger: 'Open it.' They obeyed, as if it were the most natural thing in the world.

The coffin was made of oak, and they began to unscrew the lid. The humidity of the earth had rusted the screws, and it was not without some difficulty that the coffin was opened. A painful odour arose in spite of the aromatic plants with which it was covered.

'O my God, my God!' murmured Armand, and turned paler than before.

Even the grave-digger drew back.

A great white shroud covered the corpse, closely outlining some of its contours. This shroud was almost completely eaten away at one end, and left one of the feet visible.

I was nearly fainting, and at the moment of writing these lines I see the whole scene over again in all its imposing reality.

'Quick,' said the inspector. Thereupon one of the men put out his hand, began to unscrew the shroud, and taking hold of it by one end suddenly laid bare the face of Marguerite.

It was terrible to see, it is horrible to relate. The eyes were nothing but two holes, the lips had disappeared, vanished, and the white teeth were tightly set. The black hair, long and dry, was pressed tightly about the forehead, and half veiled the green hollows of the cheeks; and yet I recognized in this face the joyous white and rose face that I had seen so often.

Armand, unable to turn away his eyes, had put the handkerchief to his mouth and bit it.

For my part, it was as if a circle of iron tightened about my head, a veil covered my eyes, a rumbling filled my ears, and all I could do was to unstop a smelling bottle which I happened to have with me, and to draw in long breaths of it.

Through this bewilderment I heard the inspector say to Duval, 'Do you identify?'

'Yes,' replied the young man in a dull voice.

'Then fasten it up and take it away,' said the inspector.

The grave-diggers put back the shroud over the face of the corpse, fastened up the coffin, took hold of each end of it, and began to carry it toward the place where they had been told to take it.

Armand did not move. His eyes were fixed upon the empty grave; he was as white as the corpse which he had just seen. He looked as if he had been turned to stone.

I saw what was coming as soon as the pain caused by the spectacle should have abated and thus ceased to sustain him. I went up to the inspector. 'Is this gentleman's presence still necessary?' I said, pointing to Armand.

'No,' he replied, 'and I should advise you to take him away. He looks ill.'

'Come,' I said to Armand, taking him by the arm.

'What?' he said, looking at me as if he did not recognize me.

'It is all over,' I added. 'You must come, my friend; you are quite white, you are cold. These emotions will be too much for you.'

'You are right. Let us go,' he answered mechanically, but without moving a step.

I took him by the arm and led him along. He let himself be guided like a child, only from time to time murmuring, 'Did you see her eyes?' and he turned as if the vision had recalled her.

Nevertheless, his steps became more irregular; he seemed to walk by a series of jerks; his teeth chattered; his hands were cold; a violent agitation ran through his body. I spoke to him; he did not answer. He was just able to let himself be led along. A cab was waiting at the gate. It was only just in time. Scarcely had he seated himself, when the shivering became more violent, and he had an actual attack of nerves, in the midst of which his fear of frightening me made him press my hand and whisper: 'It is nothing, nothing. I want to weep.'

His chest laboured, his eyes were injected with blood, but no tears came. I made him smell the salts which I had with me, and when we reached his house only the shivering remained.

With the help of his servant I put him to bed, lit a big fire in his room, and hurried off to my doctor, to whom I told all that had happened. He hastened with me.

Armand was flushed and delirious; he stammered out disconnected words, in which only the name of Marguerite could be distinctly heard.

'Well?' I said to the doctor when he had examined the patient.

'Well, he has neither more nor less than brain fever, and very lucky it is for him, for I firmly believe (God forgive me!) that he would have gone out of his mind. Fortunately, the physical malady will kill the mental one, and in a month's time he will be free from the one and perhaps from the other.'

CHAPTER VII

Illnesses like Armand's have one fortunate thing about them: they either kill outright or are very soon overcome. A fortnight after the events which I have just related, Armand was convalescent, and we had already become great friends. During the whole course of his illness I had hardly left his side.

Spring was profuse in its flowers, its leaves, its birds, its songs; and my friend's window opened gaily upon his garden, from which a reviving breath of health seemed to come to him. The doctor had allowed him to get up, and we often sat talking at the open window, at the hour when the sun is at its height, from twelve to two. I was careful not to refer to Marguerite, fearing lest the name should awaken sad recollections hidden under the apparent calm of the invalid; but Armand, on the contrary, seemed to delight in speaking of her, not as formerly, with tears in his eyes, but with a sweet smile which reassured me as to the state of his mind.

I had noticed that ever since his last visit to the cemetery, and the sight which had brought on so violent a crisis, sorrow seemed to have been overcome by sickness, and Marguerite's death no longer appeared to him under its former aspect. A kind of consolation had sprung from the certainty of which he was now fully persuaded, and in order to banish the sombre picture which often presented itself to him, he returned upon the happy recollections of his *liaison* with Marguerite, and seemed resolved to think of nothing else.

The body was too much weakened by the attack of fever, and even by the process of its cure, to permit him any violent emotions, and the universal joy of spring which wrapped him round carried his thoughts instinctively to images of joy. He had always obstinately refused to tell his family of the danger which he had been in, and when he was well again his father did not even know that he had been ill.

One evening we had sat at the window later than usual; the weather had been superb, and the sun sank to sleep in a twilight dazzling with gold and azure. Though we were in Paris, the verdure which surrounded us seemed to shut us off from the world, and our conversation was only now and again disturbed by the sound of a passing vehicle.

'It was about this time of the year, on the evening of a day like this, that I first met Marguerite,' said Armand to me, as if he were listening to his own thoughts rather than to what I was saying. I did not answer. Then turning toward me, he said:

'I must tell you the whole story; you will make a book out of it; no one will believe it, but it will perhaps be interesting to do.'

'You will tell me about it later on, my friend,' I said to him; 'you are not strong enough yet.'

'It is a warm evening, I have eaten my ration of chicken,' he said to me smiling; 'I have no fever, we have nothing to do, I will tell it to you now.'

'Since you really wish it, I will listen.'

This is what he told me, and I have scarcely changed a word of the touching story.

Yes (Armand went on, letting his head sink back on the chair), yes, it was just such an evening as this. I had spent the day in the country with one of my friends Gaston R—. We returned to Paris in the evening, and not knowing what to do we went to the Variétés. We went out during one of the *entr'actes*, and a tall woman passed us in the corridor, to whom my friend had bowed.

'Whom are you bowing to?' I asked.

'Marguerite Gautier,' he said.

'She seems much changed, for I did not recognize her,' I said with an emotion that you will soon understand.

'She has been ill; the poor girl won't last long.'

I remember the words as if they had been spoken to me yesterday.

I must tell you, my friend, that for two years the sight of this girl had made a strange impression on me whenever I came across her. Without knowing why, I turned pale and my heart beat violently. I have a friend who studies the occult sciences, and he would call what I experienced 'the affinity of fluids'; as for me, I only know that I was fated to fall in love with Marguerite, and that I foresaw it.

It is certainly the fact that she made a very definite impression upon me, that many of my friends had noticed it and that they had been much amused when they saw who it was that made this impression upon me.

The first time I ever saw her was in the Place de la Bourse, outside Susse's; an open carriage was stationed there, and a woman dressed in white got down from it. A murmur of admiration greeted her as she entered the shop. As for me, I was riveted to the spot from the moment she went in till the moment when she came out again. I could see her through the shop windows selecting what she had come to buy. I might have gone in, but I dared not. I did not know who she was, and I was afraid lest she should guess why I had come in and be offended. Nevertheless, I did not think I should ever see her again.

She was elegantly dressed; she wore a muslin dress with many flounces, an Indian shawl embroidered at the corners with gold and silk flowers, a straw hat, a single bracelet, and a heavy gold chain, such as was just then beginning to be the fashion.

She returned to her carriage and drove away. One of the shopmen stood at the door looking after his elegant customer's carriage. I went up to him and asked him what was the lady's name.

'Mademoiselle Marguerite Gautier,' he replied. I dared not ask him for her address, and went on my way.

The recollection of this vision, for it was really a vision, would not leave my mind like so many visions I had seen, and I looked everywhere for the royally beautiful woman in white.

A few days later there was a great performance at the Opéra Comique. The first person I saw in one of the boxes was Marguerite Gautier.

The young man whom I was with recognized her immediately, for he said to me, mentioning her name: 'Look at that pretty girl.'

At that moment Marguerite turned her opera-glass in our direction and, seeing my friend, smiled and beckoned to him to come to her.

'I will go and say "How do you do?" to her,' he said, 'and will be back in a moment.'

I could not help saying 'Happy man!'

'Why?'

'To go and see that woman.'

'Are you in love with her?'

'No,' I said, flushing, for I really did not know what to say; 'but I should very much like to know her.'

'Come with me. I will introduce you.'

'Ask her if you may.'

'Really, there is no need to be particular with her; come.'

What he said troubled me. I feared to discover that Marguerite was not worthy of the sentiment which I felt for her.

In a book of Alphonse Karr, entitled Am Rauchen, there is a man who one evening follows a very elegant woman, with whom he had fallen in love at first sight on account of her beauty. Only to kiss her hand he feels that he has the strength to undertake anything, the will to conquer anything, the courage to achieve anything. He scarcely dares glance at the trim ankle which she shows as she holds her dress out of the mud. While he is dreaming of all that he would do to possess this woman, she stops at the corner of the street and asks if he will come home with her. He turns his head, crosses the street, and goes back sadly to his own house.

I recalled the story, and, having longed to suffer for this woman, I was afraid that she would accept me too promptly and give me at once what I would fain have purchased by long waiting or some great sacrifice. We men are built like that; and it is very fortunate that the imagination lends much poetry to the senses, and that the desires of the body make this much concession to the dreams of the soul. If any one had said to me, You shall have this woman tonight and be killed tomorrow, I would have accepted. If any one had said to me, You can be her lover for fifty dollars, I would have refused. I would have cried like a child who sees the castle he has been dreaming about vanish away as he awakens from sleep.

All the same, I wished to know her; it was my only means of making up my mind about her. I therefore said to my friend that I insisted on having her permission to be introduced to her, and I wandered to and fro in the corridors, saying to myself that in a moment's time she was going to see me, and that I should not know which way to look. I tried (sublime childishness of love!) to string together the words I should say to her.

A moment after my friend returned. 'She is expecting us,' he said.

'Is she alone?' I asked.

'With another woman.'

'There are no men?'

'No.'

'Come, then.'

My friend went toward the door of the theatre.

'That is not the way,' I said.

'We must go and get some sweets. She asked me for some.'

We went into a confectioner's in the passage de l'Opéra. I would have bought the whole shop, and I was looking about to see what sweets to choose, when my friend asked for a pound of candied raisins.

'Do you know if she likes them?'

'She eats no other kind of sweets; everybody knows it.'

'Ah,' he went on when we had left the shop, 'do you know what kind of woman it is that I am going to introduce you to? Don't imagine it is a duchess. It is simply a kept woman, very much kept, my dear fellow; don't be shy, say anything that comes into your head.'

'Yes, yes,' I stammered, and I followed him, saying to myself that I should soon cure myself of my passion.

When I entered the box Marguerite was in fits of laughter. I would rather that she had been sad. My friend introduced me; Marguerite gave me a little nod, and said, 'And my sweets?'

'Here they are.'

She looked at me as she took them. I dropped my eyes and blushed.

She leaned across to her neighbour and said something in her ear, at which both laughed. Evidently I was the cause of their mirth, and my embarrassment increased. At that time I had as mistress a very affectionate and sentimental little person, whose sentiment and whose melancholy letters amused me greatly. I realized the pain I must have given her by what I now experienced, and for five minutes I loved her as no woman was ever loved.

Marguerite ate her candied raisins without taking any more notice of me. The friend who had introduced me did not wish to let me remain in so ridiculous a position.

'Marguerite,' he said, 'you must not be surprised if M. Duval says nothing: you overwhelm him to such a degree that he can not find a word to say.'

'I should say, on the contrary, that he has only come with you because it would have bored you to come here by yourself.'

'If that were true,' I said, 'I should not have begged Ernest to ask your permission to introduce me.'

'Perhaps that was only in order to put off the fatal moment.'

However little one may have known women like Marguerite, one can not but know the delight they take in pretending to be witty and in teasing the people whom they meet for the first time. It is no doubt a return for the humiliations which they often have to submit to on the part of those whom they see every day.

To answer them properly, one requires a certain knack, and I had not had the opportunity of acquiring it; besides, the idea that I had formed of Marguerite accentuated the effects of her mockery. Nothing that came from her was indifferent to me. I rose to my feet, saying in an altered voice, which I could not entirely control:

'If that is what you think of me, madame, I have only to ask your pardon for my indiscretion, and to take leave of you with the assurance that it shall not occur again.'

Thereupon I bowed and quitted the box. I had scarcely closed the door when I heard a third peal of laughter. It would not have been well for anybody who had elbowed me at that moment.

I returned to my seat. The signal for raising the curtain was given. Ernest came back to his place beside me.

'What a way you behaved!' he said, as he sat down. 'They will think you are mad.'

'What did Marguerite say after I had gone?'

'She laughed, and said she had never seen any one so funny. But don't look upon it as a lost chance; only do not do these women the honour of taking them seriously. They do not know what politeness and ceremony are. It is as if you were to offer perfumes to dogs – they would think it smelled bad, and go and roll in the gutter.'

'After all, what does it matter to me?' I said, affecting to speak in a nonchalant way. 'I shall never see this woman again, and if I liked her before meeting her, it is quite different now that I know her.'

'Bah! I don't despair of seeing you one day at the back of her box, and of hearing that you are ruining yourself for her. However, you are right, she hasn't been well brought up; but she would be a charming mistress to have.'

Happily, the curtain rose and my friend was silent. I could not possibly tell you what they were acting. All that I remember is that from time to time I raised my eyes to the box I had quitted so abruptly, and the faces of fresh visitors succeeded one another all the time.

I was far from having given up thinking about Marguerite. Another feeling had taken possession of me. It seemed to me that I had her insult and my absurdity to wipe out; I said to myself that if I spent every penny I had, I would win her and win my right to the place I had abandoned so quickly.

Before the performance was over Marguerite and her friend left their box. I rose from my seat.

'Are you going?' said Ernest.

'Yes.'

'Why?'

At that moment he saw that the box was empty.

'Go, go,' he said, 'and good luck, or rather better luck.'

I went out.

I heard the rustle of dresses, the sound of voices, on the staircase. I stood aside, and, without being seen, saw the two women pass me, accompanied by two young men. At the entrance to the theatre they were met by a footman.

'Tell the coachman to wait at the door of the Café Anglais,' said Marguerite. 'We will walk there.'

A few minutes afterward I saw Marguerite from the street at a window of one of the large rooms of the restaurant, pulling the camellias of her bouquet to pieces, one by one. One of the two men was leaning over her shoulder and whispering in her ear.

I took up my position at the Maison d'Or, in one of the first-floor rooms, and did not lose sight of the window for an instant. At one in the morning Marguerite got into her carriage with her three friends. I took a cab and followed them. The carriage stopped at No. 9, Rue d'Antin. Marguerite got out and went in alone. It was no doubt a mere chance, but the chance filled me with delight.

From that time forward, I often met Marguerite at the théâtre or in the Champs-Élysées. Always there was the same gaiety in her, the same emotion in me.

At last a fortnight passed without me meeting her. I met Gaston and asked after her.

'Poor girl, she is very ill,' he answered.

'What is the matter?'

'She is consumptive, and the sort of life she leads isn't exactly the thing to cure her. She has taken to her bed; she is dying.'

The heart is a strange thing; I was almost glad at hearing it.

Every day I went to ask after her, without leaving my name or my card. I heard she was convalescent and had gone to Bagnères.

Time went by, the impression, if not the memory, faded gradually from my mind. I travelled; love affairs, habits, work, took the place of other thoughts, and when I recalled this adventure I looked upon it as one of those passions which one has when one is very young, and laughs at soon afterward.

For the rest, it was no credit to me to have got the better of this recollection, for I had completely lost sight of Marguerite, and, as I told you, when she passed me in the corridor of the Variétés, I did not recognize her. She was veiled, it is true; but, veiled though she might have been two years earlier, I should not have needed to see her in order to recognize her: I should have know her intuitively. All the same, my heart began to beat when I knew that it was she; and the two years that had passed since I saw her, and what had seemed to be the results of that separation, vanished in smoke at the mere touch of her dress.

CHAPTER VIII

However (continued Armand after a pause), while I knew myself to be still in love with her, I felt more sure of myself, and part of my desire to speak to Marguerite again was a wish to make her see that I was stronger than she.

How many ways does the heart take, how many reasons does it invent for itself, in order to arrive at what it wants!

I could not remain in the corridor, and I returned to my place in the stalls, looking hastily around to see what box she was in. She was in a ground-floor box, quite alone. She had changed, as I have told you, and no longer wore an indifferent smile on her lips. She had suffered; she was still suffering. Though it was April, she was still wearing a winter costume, all wrapped up in furs.

I gazed at her so fixedly that my eyes attracted hers. She looked at me for a few seconds, put up her opera-glass to see me better, and seemed to think she recognized me, without being quite sure who I was, for when she put down her glasses, a smile, that charming feminine salutation, flitted across her lips, as if to answer the bow which she seemed to expect; but I did not respond, so as to have an advantage over her, as if I had forgotten, while she remembered. Supposing herself mistaken, she looked away. The curtain went up. I have often seen Marguerite at the theatre. I never saw her pay the slightest attention to what was being acted. As for me, the performance interested me equally little, and I paid no attention to anything but her, though doing my utmost to keep her from noticing it.

Presently I saw her glancing across at the person who was in the opposite box; on looking, I saw a woman with whom I was quite familiar. She had once been a kept woman, and had tried to go on the stage, had failed, and, relying on her acquaintance with fashionable people in Paris, gone into business and taken a milliner's shop. I saw in her a means of meeting with Marguerite, and profited by a moment in which she looked my way to wave my hand to her. As I expected, she beckoned to me to come to her box.

Prudence Duvernoy (that was the milliner's auspicious name) was one of those fat women of forty with whom one requires very little diplomacy to make them understand what one wants to know, especially when what one wants to know is as simple as what I had to ask of her.

I took advantage of a moment when she was smiling across at Marguerite to ask her, 'Whom are you looking at?'

'Marguerite Gautier.'

'You know her?'

'Yes, I am her milliner, and she is a neighbour of mine.'

'Do you live in the Rue d'Antin?'

'No. 7. The window of her dressing-room looks on to the window of mine.'

'They say she is a charming girl.'

'Don't you know her?'

'No, but I should like to.'

'Shall I ask her to come over to our box?'

'No, I would rather for you to introduce me to her.'

'At her own house?'

'Yes.'

'That is more difficult.'

'Why?'

'Because she is under the protection of a jealous old duke.'

'"Protection" is charming.'

'Yes, protection,' replied Prudence. 'Poor old man, he would be greatly embarrassed to offer her anything else.'

Prudence then told me how Marguerite had made the acquaintance of the duke at Bagnères.

'That, then,' I continued, 'is why she is alone here?'

'Precisely.'

'But who will see her home?'

'He will.'

'He will come for her?'

'In a moment.'

'And you, who is seeing you home?'

'No one.'

'May I offer myself?'

'But you are with a friend, are you not?'

'May we offer, then?'

'Who is your friend?'

'A charming fellow, very amusing. He will be delighted to make your acquaintance.'

'Well, all right; we will go after this piece is over, for I know the last piece.'

'With pleasure; I will go and tell my friend.'

'Go, then. Ah,' added Prudence, as I was going, 'there is the duke just coming into Marguerite's box.'

I looked at him. A man of about seventy had sat down behind her, and was giving her a bag of sweets, into which she dipped at once, smiling. Then she held it out toward Prudence, with a gesture which seemed to say, 'Will you have some?'

'No,' signalled Prudence.

Marguerite drew back the bag, and, turning, began to talk with the duke.

It may sound childish to tell you all these details, but everything relating to Marguerite is so fresh in my memory that I can not help recalling them now.

I went back to Gaston and told him of the arrangement I had made for him and for me. He agreed, and we left our stalls to go round to Mme. Duvernoy's box. We had scarcely opened the door leading into the stalls when we had to stand aside to allow Marguerite and the duke to pass. I would have given ten years of my life to have been in the old man's place.

When they were in the street he handed her into a phaeton, which he drove himself, and they were whirled away by two superb horses.

We returned to Prudence's box, and when the play was over we took a cab and drove to 7, Rue d'Antin. At the door, Prudence asked us to come up and see her showrooms, which we had never seen, and of which she seemed very proud. You can imagine how eagerly I accepted. It seemed to me as if I was coming nearer and nearer to Marguerite. I soon turned the conversation in her direction.

'The old duke is at your neighbour's?' I said to Prudence.

'Oh, no; she is probably alone.'

'But she must be dreadfully bored,' said Gaston.

'We spend most of our evenings together, or she calls to me when she comes in. She never goes to bed before two in the morning. She can't sleep before that.'

'Why?'

'Because she suffers in the chest, and is almost always feverish.'

'Hasn't she any lovers?'

'I never see any one remain after I leave; I don't say no one ever comes when I am gone. Often in the evening I meet there a certain Comte de N., who thinks he is making some headway by calling on her at eleven in the evening, and by sending her jewels to any extent; but she can't stand him. She makes a mistake; he is very rich. It is in vain that I say to her from time to time, "My dear child, there's the man for you." She who generally listens to me, turns her back and replies that he is too stupid. Stupid, indeed, he is; but it would be a position for her, when this old duke might die any day. Old men are egoists; his family are always reproaching him for his affection for Marguerite; there are two reasons why he is likely to leave her nothing. I give her good advice, and she only says it will be plenty of time to take on the count when the duke's dead.'

'It isn't all fun,' continued Prudence, 'to live like that. I know very well it wouldn't suit me, and I should soon send the old man about his business. He is so dull; he calls her his daughter; looks after her like a child; and is always in the way. I am sure at this very moment one of his servants is prowling about in the street to see who comes out, and especially who goes in.'

'Ah, poor Marguerite!' said Gaston, sitting down to the piano and playing a waltz. 'I hadn't a notion of it, but I did notice she hasn't been looking so gay lately.'

'Hush,' said Prudence, listening. Gaston stopped.

'She is calling me, I think.'

We listened. A voice was calling, 'Prudence!'

'Come, now, you must go,' said Mme. Duvernoy.

'Ah, that is your idea of hospitality,' said Gaston, laughing, 'we won't go till we please.'

'Why should we go?'

'I am going over to Marguerite's.'

'We will wait here.'

'You can't.'

'Then we will go with you.'

'That still less.'

'I know Marguerite,' said Gaston; 'I can very well pay her a call.'

'But Armand doesn't know her.'

'I will introduce him.'

'Impossible.'

We again heard Marguerite's voice calling to Prudence, who rushed to her dressing-room window. I followed with Gaston as she opened the window. We hid ourselves so as not to be seen from outside.

'I have been calling you for ten minutes,' said Marguerite from her window, in almost an imperious tone of voice.

'What do you want?'

'I want you to come over at once.'

'Why?'

'Because the Comte de N. is still here, and he is boring me to death.'

'I can't now.'

'What is hindering you?'

'There are two young fellows here who won't go.'

'Tell them that you must go out.'

'I have told them.'

'Well, then, leave them in the house. They will soon go when they see you have gone.'

'They will turn everything upside down.'

'But what do they want?'

'They want to see you.'

'What are they called?'

'You know one, M. Gaston R.'

'Ah, yes, I know him. And the other?'

'M. Armand Duval; and you don't know him.'

'No, but bring them along. Anything is better than the count. I expect you. Come at once.'

Marguerite closed her window and Prudence hers. Marguerite, who had remembered my face for a moment, did not remember my name. I would rather have been remembered to my disadvantage than thus forgotten.

'I knew,' said Gaston, 'that she would be delighted to see us.'

'Delighted isn't the word,' replied Prudence, as she put on her hat and shawl. 'She will see you in order to get rid of the count. Try to be more agreeable than he is, or (I know Marguerite) she will put it all down to me.'

We followed Prudence downstairs. I trembled; it seemed to me that this visit was to have a great influence on my life. I was still more agitated than on the evening when I was introduced in the box at the Opéra Comique. As we reached the door that you know, my heart beat so violently that I was hardly able to think.

We heard the sound of a piano. Prudence rang. The piano was silent. A woman who looked more like a companion than a servant opened the door. We went into the drawing-room, and from that to the boudoir, which was then just as you have seen it since. A young man was leaning against the mantelpiece. Marguerite, seated at the piano, let her fingers wander over the notes, beginning scraps of music without finishing them. The whole scene breathed boredom, the man embarrassed by the consciousness of his nullity, the woman tired of her dismal visitor. At the voice of Prudence, Marguerite rose, and coming toward us with a look of gratitude to Mme. Duvernoy, said:

'Come in, and welcome.'

CHAPTER IX

'Good-evening, my dear Gaston,' said Marguerite to my companion. 'I am very glad to see you. Why didn't you come to see me in my box at the Variétés?'

'I was afraid it would be indiscreet.'

'Friends,' and Marguerite lingered over the word, as if to intimate to those who were present that in spite of the familiar way in which she greeted him, Gaston was not and never had been anything more than a friend, 'friends are always welcome.'

'Then, will you permit me to introduce M. Armand Duval?'

'I had already authorized Prudence to do so.'

'As far as that goes, madame,' I said, bowing, and succeeding in getting more or less intelligible sounds out of my throat, 'I have already had the honour of being introduced to you.'

Marguerite's beautiful eyes seemed to be looking back in memory, but she could not, or seemed not to, remember.

'Madame,' I continued, 'I am grateful to you for having forgotten the occasion of my first introduction, for I was very absurd and must have seemed to you very tiresome. It was at the Opéra Comique, two years ago; I was with Ernest de ——.'

'Ah, I remember,' said Marguerite, with a smile. 'It was not you who were absurd; it was I who was mischievous, as I still am, but somewhat less. You have forgiven me?'

And she held out her hand, which I kissed.

'It is true,' she went on; 'you know, I have the bad habit of trying to embarrass people the first time I meet them. It is very stupid. My doctor says it is because I am nervous and always ill; believe my doctor.'

'But you seem quite well.'

'Oh! I have been very ill.'

51

'I know.'

'Who told you?'

'Every one knew it; I often came to inquire after you, and I was happy to hear of your convalescence.'

'They never gave me your card.'

'I did not leave it.'

'Was it you, then, who called every day while I was ill, and would never leave your name?'

'Yes, it was I.'

'Then you are more than indulgent, you are generous. You, count, wouldn't have done that,' said she, turning toward M. de N., after giving me one of those looks in which women sum up their opinion of a man.

'I have only known you for two months,' replied the count.

'And this gentleman only for five minutes. You always say something ridiculous.'

Women are pitiless toward those whom they do not care for. The count reddened and bit his lips.

I was sorry for him, for he seemed, like myself, to be in love, and the bitter frankness of Marguerite must have made him very unhappy, expecially in the presence of two strangers.

'You were playing the piano when we came in,' I said, in order to change the conversation. 'Won't you be so good as to treat me as an old acquaintance and go on?'

'Oh,' said she, flinging herself on the sofa and motioning us to sit down, 'Gaston knows what my music is like. It is very well when I am alone with the count, but I won't inflict such a punishment on you.'

'You show me that preference?' said M. de N., with a smile which he tried to render delicately ironical.

'Don't reproach me for it. It is the only one.' It was fated that the poor man was not to say a single word. He cast a supplicating glance at Marguerite.

'Well, Prudence,' she went on, 'have you done what I asked you to do?'

'Yes.'

'All right. You will tell me about it later. We must talk it over; don't go before I can speak with you.'

'We are doubtless intruders,' I said, 'And now that we, or rather I, have had a second introduction, to blot out the first, it is time for Gaston and me to be going.'

'Not in the least. I didn't mean that for you. I want you to stay.'

The count took a very elegant watch out of his pocket and looked at the time. 'I must be going to my club,' he said. Marguerite did not answer. The count thereupon left his position by the fireplace and going up to her, said: 'Adieu, madame.'

Marguerite rose. 'Adieu, my dear count. Are you going already?'

'Yes, I fear I am boring you.'

'You are not boring me today more than any other day. When shall I be seeing you?'

'When you permit me.'

'Good-bye, then.'

It was cruel, you will admit. Fortunately, the count had excellent manners and was very good-tempered. He merely kissed Marguerite's hand, which she held out to him carelessly enough, and, bowing to us, went out.

As he crossed the threshold, he cast a glance at Prudence. She shrugged her shoulders, as much as to say: 'What do you expect? I have done all I could.'

'Nanine!' cried Marguerite. 'Light M. le Comte to the door.'

We heard the door open and shut.

'At last,' cried Marguerite, coming back, 'he has gone! That man gets frightfully on my nerves.'

'My dear child,' said Prudence, 'you really treat him too badly, and he is so good and kind to you. Look at this watch on the mantelpiece, that he gave you; it must have cost him at least three thousand francs, I am sure.'

And Mme. Duvernoy began to turn it over, as it lay on the mantelpiece, looking at it with covetous eyes.

'My dear,' said Marguerite, sitting down to the piano, 'when I put on one side what he gives me and on the other what he says to me, it seems to me that he buys his visits very cheap.'

'The poor fellow is in love with you.'

'If I had to listen to everybody who was in love with me, I shouldn't have time for my dinner.'

And she began to run her fingers over the piano, and then, turning to us, she said:

'What will you take? I think I should like a little punch.'

'And I could eat a little chicken,' said Prudence. 'Suppose we have supper?'

'That's it, let's go and have supper,' said Gaston.

'No, we will have supper here.'

She rang, and Nanine appeared.

'Send for some supper.'

'What must I get?'

'Whatever you like, but at once.'

Nanine went out.

'That's it,' said Marguerite, jumping like a child, 'we'll have supper. How tiresome that idiot of a count is!'

The more I saw her, the more she enchanted me. She was exquisitely beautiful. Her slenderness was a charm. I was lost in contemplation.

What was passing in my mind I should have some difficulty in explaining. I was full of indulgence for her life, full of admiration for her beauty. The proof of disinterestedness that she gave in not accepting a rich and fashionable young man, ready to waste all his money upon her, excused her in my eyes for all her faults in the past.

There was a kind of candour in this woman. You could see she was still in the virginity of vice. Her firm walk, her supple figure, her rosy, open nostrils, her large eyes, slightly tinged with blue, indicated one of those ardent natures which shed around them a sort of voluptuous perfume, like Eastern vials, which, close them as tightly as you will, still let some of their perfume escape. Finally, whether it was simple nature or a breath of fever, there passed from time to time in the eyes of this woman a glimmer of desire, giving promise of a very heaven for one whom she should love. But those who had loved Marguerite were not to be counted, nor those whom she had loved.

In this girl there was at once the virgin whom a mere nothing had turned into a courtesan, and the courtesan whom a mere nothing would have turned into the most loving and the purest of virgins. Marguerite had still pride and independence, two sentiments which, if they are wounded, can be the equivalent of a sense of shame. I did not speak a word; my soul seemed to have passed into my heart and my heart into my eyes.

'So,' said she all at once, 'it was you who came to inquire after me when I was ill?'

'Yes.'

'Do you know, it was quite splendid of you! How can I thank you for it?'

'By allowing me to come and see you from time to time.'

'As often as you like, from five to six, and from eleven to twelve. Now, Gaston, play the Invitation à la Valse.'

'Why?'

'To please me, first of all, and then because I never can manage to play it myself.'

'What part do you find difficult?'

'The third part, the part in sharps.'

Gaston rose and went to the piano, and began to play the wonderful melody of Weber, the music of which stood open before him.

Marguerite, resting one hand on the piano, followed every note of music, accompanying it in a low voice, and when Gaston had come to the passage which she had mentioned to him, she sang out, running her fingers along the top of the piano:

'Do, re, mi, do, re, fa, mi, re; that is what I can not do. Over again.'

Gaston began over again, after which Marguerite said:

'Now, let me try.'

She took her place and began to play; but her rebellious fingers always came to grief over one of the notes.

'Isn't it incredible,' she cried, exactly like a child, 'that I can not succeed in playing that passage? Would you believe that I sometimes spend two hours of the morning over it? And when I think that that idiot of a count plays it without his music, and beautifully, I really believe it is that which makes me so furious with him.'

And she began again, always with the same result.

'The devil take Weber, music, and pianos!' she cried, throwing the music to the other end of the room. 'How can I play eight sharps one after another?' She folded her arms and looked at us, stamping her foot. The blood flew to her cheeks, and her lips half opened in a slight cough.

'Come, come,' said Prudence, who had taken off her hat and was smoothing her hair before the glass, 'you will work yourself into a rage and do yourself harm. Better come and have supper; for my part, I am dying of hunger.'

Marguerite rang the bell, sat down to the piano again, and began to hum over a very bawdy song, which she accompanied without difficulty. Gaston knew the song, and they gave a sort of duet.

'Don't sing those beastly things,' I said to Marguerite, imploringly.

'Oh, how proper you are!' she said, smiling and giving me her hand.

'It is not for myself, but for you.'

Marguerite made a gesture as if to say, 'Oh, it is long since that I have done with propriety!'

At that moment Nanine appeared.

'Is supper ready?' asked Marguerite.

'Yes, madame, in one moment.'

'Apropos,' said Prudence to me, 'you have not looked round; come, and I will show you.'

As you know, the drawing-room was a marvel.

Marguerite went with us for a moment; then she called Gaston and went into the dining-room to see if supper was ready.

'Ah,' said Prudence, catching sight of a little Saxe figure on a side-table, 'I never knew you had this little gentleman.'

'Which?'

'A little shepherd holding a bird-cage.'

'Take it, if you like it.'

'I won't deprive you of it.'

'I was going to give it to my maid. I think it hideous; but if you like it, take it.'

Prudence only saw the present, not the way in which it was given. She put the little figure on one side, and took me into the dressing-room, where she showed me two miniatures hanging side by side, and said:

'That is the Comte de G., who was very much in love with Marguerite; it was he who brought her out. Do you know him?'

'No. And this one?' I inquired, pointing to the other miniature.

'That is the little Vicomte de L. He was obliged to disappear.'

'Why?'

'Because he was all but ruined. That's one, if you like, who loved Marguerite.'

'And she loved him, too, no doubt?'

'She is such a queer girl, one never knows. The night he went away she went to the theatre as usual, and yet she had cried when he said good-bye to her.'

Just then Nanine appeared, to tell us that supper was served.

When we entered the dining-room, Marguerite was leaning against the wall, and Gaston, holding her hands, was speaking to her in a low voice.

'You are mad,' replied Marguerite, 'You know quite well that I don't want you. It is no good at the end of two years to make love to a woman like me. With us, it is at once, or never. Come, gentlemen, supper!'

And, slipping away from Gaston, Marguerite made him sit on her right at table, me on her left, then called to Nanine:

'Before you sit down, tell them in the kitchen not to open to anybody if there is a ring.'

This order was given at one o'clock in the morning.

We laughed, drank, and ate freely at this supper. In a short while mirth had reached its last limit, and the words that seem funny to a certain class of people, words that degrade the mouth that utters them, were heard from time to time amidst the applause of Nanine, of Prudence, and of Marguerite. Gaston was thoroughly amused; he was a very good sort of fellow, but somewhat spoiled by the habits of his youth. For a moment I tried to forget myself, to force my heart and my thoughts to become indifferent to the sight before me, and to take my share of that gaiety which seemed like one of the courses of the meal. But little by little I withdrew from the noise; my glass remained full, and I felt almost sad as I saw this beautiful creature of twenty drinking, talking like a porter, and laughing the more loudly the more scandalous was the joke.

Nevertheless, this hilarity, this way of talking and drinking, which seemed to me in the others the mere results of bad company or of bad habits, seemed in Marguerite a necessity of forgetting, a fever, a nervous irritability. At every glass of champagne her cheeks would flush with a feverish colour, and a cough, hardly perceptible at the beginning of supper, became at last so violent that she was obliged to lean her head on the back of her chair and hold her chest in her hands every time that she coughed.

I suffered at the thought of the injury to so frail a constitution which must come from daily excesses like this. At length, something which I had feared and foreseen happened. Toward the end of supper Marguerite was seized by a more violent fit of coughing than any she had had while I was there. It seemed as if her chest were being torn in two. The poor girl turned crimson, closed her eyes under the pain, and put her napkin to her lips. It was stained with a drop of blood. She rose and ran into her dressing-room.

'What is the matter with Marguerite?' asked Gaston.

'She has been laughing too much, and she is spitting blood. Oh, it is nothing; it happens to her every day. She will be back in a minute. Leave her alone. She prefers it.'

I could not stay still; and to the consternation of Prudence and Nanine, who called me to come back, I followed Marguerite.

CHAPTER X

The room to which she had fled was lit only by a single candle.
She lay back on a great sofa, her dress undone, holding one
hand to her heart, and letting the other hang by her side. On
the table was a basin half full of water, and the water was
stained with streaks of blood.

Very pale, her mouth half open, Marguerite tried to recover
breath. Now and again her bosom was raised by a long sigh,
which seemed to relieve her a little, and for a few seconds she
would seem to be quite comfortable.

I went up to her; she made no movement, and I sat down
and took the hand which was lying on the sofa.

'Ah! it is you,' she said, with a smile.

I must have looked greatly agitated, for she added:

'Are you unwell, too?'

'No, but you: do you still suffer?'

'Very little'; and she wiped off with her handkerchief the
tears which the coughing had brought to her eyes; 'I am used
to it now.'

'You are killing yourself, madame,' I said to her in a moved
voice. 'I wish I were a friend, a relation of yours, that I might
keep you from doing yourself harm like this.'

'Ah! it is really not worth your while to alarm yourself,' she
replied in a somewhat bitter tone; 'see how much notice the
others take of me! They know too well that there is nothing to
be done.'

Thereupon she got up, and, taking the candle, put it on the
mantelpiece and looked at herself in the glass.

'How pale I am!' she said, as she fastened her dress and
passed her fingers over her loosened hair. 'Come, let us go
back to supper. Are you coming?'

I sat still and did not move.

She saw how deeply I had been affected by the whole scene,
and, coming up to me, held out her hand, saying:

'Come now, let us go.'

I took her hand, raised it to my lips, and in spite of myself two tears fell upon it.

'Why, what a child you are!' she said, sitting down by my side again. 'You are crying! What is the matter?'

'I must seem very silly to you, but I am frightfully troubled by what I have just seen.'

'You are very good! What would you have of me? I can not sleep. I must amuse myself a little. And then, girls like me, what does it matter, one more or less? The doctors tell me that the blood I spit up comes from my throat; I pretend to believe them; it is all I can do for them.'

'Listen, Marguerite,' I said, unable to contain myself any longer, 'I do not know what influence you are going to have over my life, but at this present moment there is no one, not even my sister, in whom I feel the interest which I feel in you. It has been just the same ever since I saw you. Well, for Heaven's sake, take care of yourself, and do not live as you are living now.'

'If I took care of myself I should die. All that supports me is the feverish life I lead. Then, as for taking care of oneself, that is all very well for women with families and friends; as for us, from the moment we can no longer serve the vanity or the pleasure of our lovers, they leave us, and long nights follow long days. I know it. I was in bed for two months, and after three weeks no one came to see me.'

'It is true I am nothing to you,' I went on, 'but if you will let me, I will look after you like a brother, I will never leave your side, and I will cure you. Then, when you are strong again, you can go back to the life you are leading if you choose; but I am sure you will come to prefer a quiet life, which will make you happier and keep your beauty unspoiled.'

'You think like that tonight because the wine has made you sad, but you would never have the patience that you pretend to.'

'Permit me to say, Marguerite, that you were ill for two months, and that for two months I came to ask after you every day.'

'It is true, but why did you not come up?'

'Because I did not know you then.'

'Need you have been so particular with a girl like me?'

'One must always be particular with a woman; it is what I feel, at least.'

'So you would look after me?'

'Yes.'

'You would stay by me all day?'

'Yes.'

'And even all night?'

'As long as I did not weary you.'

'And what do you call that?'

'Devotion.'

'And where does this devotion come from?'

'The irresistible sympathy which I have for you.'

'So you are in love with me? Say it straight out, it is much more simple.'

'It is possible; but if I am to say it to you one day, it is not today.'

'You will do better never to say it.'

'Why?'

'Because only two things can come of it.'

'What?'

'Either I shall not accept: then you will have a grudge against me; or I shall accept: then you will have a sorry mistress; a woman who is nervous, ill, sad, or gay with a gaiety sadder than grief, a woman who spits blood and spends a hundred thousand francs a year. That is all very well for a rich old man like the duke, but it is very bad for a young man like you, and the proof of it is that all the young lovers I have had have very soon left me.'

I did not answer; I listened. This frankness, which was almost a kind of confession, the sad life, of which I caught some glimpse through the golden veil which covered it, and whose reality the poor girl sought to escape in dissipation, drink, and wakefulness, impressed me so deeply that I could not utter a single word.

'Come,' continued Marguerite, 'We are talking mere childishness. Give me your arm and let us go back to the dining-room. They won't know what we mean by our absence.'

'Go in, if you like, but allow me to stay here.'

'Why?'

'Because your mirth hurts me.'

'Well, I will be sad.'

'Marguerite, let me say to you something which you have no doubt often heard, so often that the habit of hearing it has made you believe it no longer, but which is none the less real, and which I will never repeat.'

'And that is . . .?' she said, with the smile of a young mother listening to some foolish notion of her child.

'It is this, that ever since I have seen you, I know not why, you have taken a place in my life; that, if I drive the thought of you out of my mind, it always comes back; that when I met you today, after not having seen you for two years, you made a deeper impression on my heart and mind than ever; that, now that you have let me come to see you, now that I know you, now that I know all that is strange in you, you have become a necessity of my life, and you will drive me mad, not only if you will not love me, but if you will not let me love you.'

'But foolish creature that you are, I shall say to you, like Mme. D., "You must be very rich, then!" Why, don't you know that I spend six or seven thousand francs a month, and that I could not live without it; you don't know, my poor friend, that I should ruin you in no time, and that your family would cast you off if you were to live with a woman like me. Let us be friends, good friends, but no more. Come and see me, we will laugh and talk, but don't exaggerate what I am worth, for I am worth very little. You have a good heart, you want some one to love you, you are too young and too sensitive to live in a world like mine. Take a married woman. You see, I speak to you frankly, like a friend.'

'But what the devil are you doing there?' cried Prudence, who had come in without our hearing her, and who now stood just inside the door, and with her hair half coming down and her dress undone. I recognized the hand of Gaston.

'We are talking sense,' said Marguerite; 'leave us alone; we will be back soon.'

'Good, good! Talk, my children,' said Prudence, going out and closing the door behind her, as if to further emphasize the tone in which she had said these words.

'Well, it is agreed,' continued Marguerite, when we were alone, 'you won't fall in love with me?'

'I will go away.'

'So much as that?'

I had gone too far to draw back; and I was really carried away. This mingling of gaiety, sadness, candour, prostitution, her very malady, which no doubt developed in her a sensitiveness to impressions, as well as an irritability of nerves, all this made it clear to me that if from the very beginning I did not completely dominate her light and forgetful nature, she was lost to me.

'Come, now, do you seriously mean what you say?'

'Seriously.'

'But why didn't you say it to me sooner?'

'When could I have said it?'

'The day after you had been introduced to me at the Opéra Comique.'

'I thought you would have received me very badly if I had come to see you.'

'Why?'

'Because I had behaved so stupidly.'

'That's true. And yet you were already in love with me.'

'Yes.'

'And that didn't hinder you from going to bed and sleeping quite comfortably. One knows what that sort of love means.'

'There you are mistaken. Do you know what I did that evening, after the Opéra Comique?'

'No.'

'I waited for you at the door of the Café Anglais. I followed the carriage in which you and your three friends were, and when I saw you were the only one to get down, and that you went in alone, I was very happy.'

Marguerite began to laugh.

'What are you laughing at?'

'Nothing.'

'Tell me, I beg of you, or I shall think you are still laughing at me.'

'You won't be cross?'

'What right have I to be cross?'

'Well, there was sufficient reason why I went in alone.'

'What?'

'Some one was waiting for me here.'

If she had thrust a knife into me she would not have hurt me more. I rose, and holding out my hand. 'Good-bye,' said I.

'I knew you would be cross,' she said; 'men are frantic to know what is certain to give them pain.'

'But I assure you,' I added coldly, as if wishing to prove how completely I was cured of my passion, 'I assure you that I am not cross. It was quite natural that some one should be waiting for you, just as it is quite natural that I should go from here at three in the morning.'

'Have you, too, some one waiting for you?'

'No, but I must go.'

'Good-bye, then.'

'You send me away?'

'Not the least in the world.'

'Why are you so unkind to me?'

'How have I been unkind to you?'

'In telling me that some one was waiting for you.'

'I could not help laughing at the idea that you had been so happy to see me come in alone when there was such a good reason for it.'

'One finds pleasure in childish enough things, and it is too bad to destroy such a pleasure when, by simply leaving it alone, one can make somebody so happy?'

'But what do you think I am? I am neither maid nor duchess. I didn't know you till today, and I am not responsible to you for my actions. Supposing one day I should become your mistress, you are bound to know that I have had other lovers besides you. If you make scenes of jealousy like this before, what will it be after, if that after should ever exist? I never met any one like you.'

'That is because no one has ever loved you as I love you.'

'Frankly, then, you really love me?'

'As much as it is possible to love, I think.'

'And that has lasted since —?'

'Since the day I saw you go into Susse's three years ago.'

'Do you know, that is tremendously fine? Well what am I to do in return?'

'Love me a little,' I said, my heart beating so that I could hardly speak; for, in spite of the half-mocking smiles with which she had accompanied the whole conversation, it seemed to me that Marguerite began to share my agitation, and that the hour so long awaited was drawing near.

'Well, but the duke?'

'What duke?'

'My jealous old duke.'

'He will know nothing.'

'And if he should?'

'He would forgive you.'

'Ah, no, he would leave me, and what would become of me?'

'You risk that for some one else.'

'How do you know?'

'By the order you gave not to admit any one tonight.'

'It is true; but that is a serious friend.'

'For whom you care nothing, as you have shut your door against him at such an hour.'

'It is not for you to reproach me, since it was in order to receive you, and your friend.'

Little by little I had drawn nearer to Marguerite. I had put my arms about her waist, and I felt her supple body weigh lightly on my clasped hands.

'If you knew how much I love you!' I said in a low voice.

'Really true?'

'I swear it.'

'Well, if you will promise to do everything I tell you, without a word, without an opinion, without a question, perhaps I will say yes.'

'I will do everything you wish!'

'But I forewarn you I must be free to do as I please, without giving you the slightest details what I do. I have long wished for a young lover, who should be young and not self-willed, loving without distrust, loved without claiming the right to it. I have never found one. Men, instead of being satisfied in obtaining for a long time what they scarcely hoped to obtain once, exact from their mistresses a full account of the present, the past, and even the future. As they get accustomed to her, they want to rule her, and the more one gives them the more exacting they become. If I decide now on taking a new lover, he must have three very rare qualities: he must be confiding, submissive, and discreet.'

'Well, I will be all that you wish.'

'We shall see.'

'When shall we see?'

'Later on.'

'Why?'

'Because,' said Marguerite, releasing herself from my arms, and, taking from a great bunch of red camellias a single camellia, she placed it in my buttonhole, 'because one can not always carry out agreements the day they are signed.'

'And when shall I see you again?' I said, clasping her in my arms.

'When this camellia changes colour.'

'When will it change colour?'

'Tomorrow night between eleven and twelve. Are you satisfied?'

'Need you ask me?'

'Not a word of this either to your friend or to Prudence, or to anybody whatever.'

'I promise.'

'Now, kiss me, and we will go back to the dining-room.'

She held up her lips to me, smoothed her hair again, and we went out of the room, she singing, and I almost beside myself.

In the next room she stopped for a moment and said to me in a low voice:

'It must seem strange to you that I am ready to take you at a moment's notice. Shall I tell you why? It is,' she continued, taking my hand and placing it against her heart so that I could feel how rapidly and violently it palpitated; 'it is because I shall not live as long as others, and I have promised myself to live more quickly.'

'Don't speak to me like that, I entreat you.'

'Oh, make yourself easy,' she continued, laughing; 'however short a time I have to live, I shall live longer than you will love me!'

And she went singing into the dining-room.

'Where is Nanine?' she said, seeing Gaston and Prudence alone.

'She is asleep in your room, waiting till you are ready to go to bed,' replied Prudence.

'Poor thing, I am killing her! And now, gentlemen, it is time to go.'

Ten minutes after, Gaston and I left the house. Marguerite shook hands with me and said good-bye. Prudence remained behind.

'Well,' said Gaston, when we were in the street, 'what do you think of Marguerite?'

'She is an angel, and I am madly in love with her.'

'So I guessed; did you tell her so?'

'Yes.'

'And did she promise to believe you?'

'No.'

'She is not like Prudence.'

'Did she promise to?'

'Better still, my dear fellow. You wouldn't think it; but she is still not half bad, poor old Duvernoy!'

CHAPTER XI

At this point Armand stopped.

'Would you close the window for me?' he said. 'I am beginning to feel cold. Meanwhile, I will get into bed.'

I closed the window. Armand, who was still very weak, took off his dressing-gown and lay down in bed resting his head for a few moments on the pillow, like a man who is tired by much talking or disturbed by painful memories.

'Perhaps you have been talking too much,' I said to him. 'Would you rather for me to go and leave you to sleep? You can tell me the rest of the story another day.'

'Are you tired of listening to it?'

'Quite the contrary.'

'Then I will go on. If you left me alone, I should not sleep.'

When I returned home (he continued, without needing to pause and recollect himself, so fresh were all the details in his mind), I did not go to bed, but began to reflect over the day's adventure. The meeting, the introduction, the promise of Marguerite, had followed one another so rapidly, and so unexpectedly, that there were moments when it seemed to me I had been dreaming. Nevertheless, it was not the first time that a girl like Marguerite had promised herself to a man on the morrow of the day on which he had asked for the promise.

Though, indeed, I made this reflection, the first impression produced on me by my future mistress was so strong that it still persisted. I refused obstinately to see in her a woman like other women, and, with the vanity so common to all men, I was ready to believe that she could not but share the attraction which drew me to her.

Yet, I had before me plenty of instances to the contrary, and I had often heard that the affection of Marguerite was a thing to be had more or less dear, according to the season.

But, on the other hand, how was I to reconcile this reputation with her constant refusal of the young count whom we had found at her house? You may say that he was unattractive to her, and that, as she was splendidly kept by the duke, she would be more likely to choose a man who was attractive to her, if she were to take another lover. If so, why did she not choose Gaston, who was rich, witty and charming, and why did she care for me, whom she had thought so ridiculous the first time she had seen me?

It is true that there are events of a moment which tell more than a courtship of a year. Of those who were at the supper, I was the only one who had been concerned at her leaving the table. I had followed her, I had been so affected as to be unable to hide it from her, I had wept as I kissed her hand. This circumstance, added to my daily visits during the two months of her illness, might have shown her that I was somewhat different from the other men she knew, and perhaps she had said to herself that for a love which could thus manifest itself she might well do what she had done so often that it had no more consequence for her.

All these suppositions, as you may see, were improbable enough; but whatever might have been the reason of her consent, one thing was certain, she had consented.

Now, I was in love with Marguerite. I had nothing more to ask of her. Nevertheless, though she was only a kept woman, I had so anticipated for myself, perhaps, to poetize it a little, a hopeless love, that the nearer the moment approached when I should have nothing more to hope, the more I doubted. I did not close my eyes all night.

I scarcely knew myself. I was half demented. Now, I seemed to myself not handsome or rich or elegant enough to possess such a woman, now I was filled with vanity at the thought of it; then I began to fear lest Marguerite had no more than a few days caprice for me, and I said to myself that since we should soon have to part, it would be better not to keep her appointment, but to write and tell her my fears and leave her. From that I went on to unlimited hope, unbounded confidence. I dreamed incredible dreams of the future; I said to myself that she should owe to me her moral and physical recovery, that I should spend my whole life with her, and that her love should make me happier than all the maidenly loves in the world.

But I can not repeat to you the thousand thoughts that rose from my heart to my head, and that only faded away with the sleep that came to me at daybreak.

When I awoke it was two o'clock. The weather was superb. I don't think life ever seemed to me so beautiful and so full of possibilities. The memories of the night before came to me without shadow or hindrance, escorted gaily by the hopes of the night to come. From time to time my heart leaped with love and joy in my breast. A sweet fever thrilled me. I thought no more of the reasons which had filled my mind before I slept. I saw only the result, I thought only of the hour when I was to see Marguerite again.

It was impossible to stay indoors. My room seemed too small to contain my happiness. I needed the whole of Nature to unbosom myself.

I went out. Passing by the Rue d'Antin, I saw Marguerite's coupé waiting for her at the door. I went toward the Champs-Élysées. I loved all the people whom I met. Love gives one a kind of goodness.

After I had been walking for an hour from the Marly horses to the Rond-Point, I saw Marguerite's carriage in the distance; I divined rather than recognized it. As it was turning the corner of the Champs-Élysées it stopped, and a tall young man left a group of people with whom he was talking and came up to her. They talked for a few moments; the young man returned to his friends, the horses set out again, and as I came near the group I recognized the one who had spoken to Marguerite as the Comte de G., whose portrait I had seen and whom Prudence had indicated to me as the man to whom Marguerite owed her position. It was to him that she had closed her doors the night before; I imagined that she had stopped her carriage in order to explain to him why she had done so, and I hoped that at the same time she had found some new pretext for not receiving him on the following night.

How I spent the rest of the day I do not know; I walked, smoked, talked, but what I said, whom I met, I had utterly forgotten by ten o'clock in the evening.

All I remember is that when I returned home, I spent three hours over my toilet, and I looked at my watch and my clock a hundred times, which unfortunately both pointed to the same hour.

When it struck half past ten, I said to myself that it was time to go.

I lived at that time in the Rue de Provence; I followed the Rue du Mont-Blanc, crossed the Boulevard, went up the Rue Louis-le-Grand, the Rue de Port-Mahon, and the Rue d'Antin. I looked up at Marguerite's windows. There was a light. I rang. I asked the porter if Mlle. Gautier was at home. He replied that she never came in before eleven or a quarter past eleven. I looked at my watch. I intended to come quite slowly, and I had come in five minutes from the Rue de Provence to the Rue d'Antin.

I walked to and fro in the street; there are no shops, and at that hour it is quite deserted. In half an hour's time Marguerite arrived. She looked around her as she got down from her coupé, as if looking for some one. The carriage drove off; the stables were not at the house. Just as Marguerite was going to ring, I went up to her and said, 'Good-evening.'

'Ah, it is you,' she said, in a tone that by no means reassured me as to her pleasure in seeing me.

'Did you not promise me that I might come and see you today?'

'Quite right. I had forgotten.'

This word upset all the reflections I had made in the morning, and all the hopes I had had during the day. Nevertheless, I was beginning to get used to her ways, and I did not leave her, as I should certainly have done once. We entered. Nanine had already opened the door.

'Has Prudence come?' said Marguerite.

'No, madame.'

'Say that she is to be admitted as soon as she comes. But first put out the lamp in the drawing-room, and if any one comes, say that I have not come back and shall not be coming back.'

She was like a woman who is preoccupied with something, and perhaps annoyed by an unwelcome guest. I did not know what to do or say. Marguerite went toward her bedroom; I remained where I was.

'Come,' she said.

She took off her hat and her velvet cloak and threw them on the bed, then let herself drop into a great armchair beside the fire, which she kept till the very beginning of summer, and said to me as she fingered her watch chain:

'Well, what news have you got for me?'

'None, except that I ought not to have come tonight.'

'Why?'

'Because you seemed vexed, and no doubt I am boring you.'

'You are not boring me; only I am not well; I have been suffering all day. I could not sleep and I have a frightful headache.'

'Shall I go away and let you go to bed?'

'Oh, you can stay. If I want to go to bed I don't mind your being there.'

At that moment there was a ring.

'Who is coming now?' she said, with an impatient movement.

A few minutes after there was another ring.

'Isn't there any one to go to the door? I shall have to go myself.'

She got up and said to me, 'Wait here.'

She went through the rooms, and I heard her open the outer door. I listened.

The person whom she had admitted did not come farther than the dining-room. At the first word I recognized the voice of the young Comte de N.

'How are you this evening?'

'Not well,' replied Marguerite drily.

'Am I disturbing you?'

'Perhaps.'

'How you receive me! What have I done, my dear Marguerite?'

'My dear friend, you have done nothing. I am ill; I must go to bed, so you will be good enough to go. It is sickening not to be able to return at night without you making your appearance five minutes afterward. What is it you want? For me to be your mistress? Well, I have already told you a hundred times, No; you simply worry me, and you might as well go somewhere else. I repeat to you today, for the last time, I don't want anything to do with you; that's settled. Good-bye. Here's Nanine coming in; she can light you to the door. Good-night.'

Without adding another word, or listening to what the young man stammered out, Marguerite returned to the room and slammed the door. Nanine entered a moment after.

'Now understand,' said Marguerite, 'you are always to say to that idiot that I am not in, or that I will not see him. I am tired out with seeing people who always want the same thing; who pay me for it, and then think they are quit of me. If those who are going to go in for our hateful business only knew what it really was they would sooner be chambermaids. But no, vanity, the desire of having dresses and carriages and diamonds carries us away; one believes what one hears, for here, as elsewhere, there is such a thing as belief, and one uses up one's heart, one's body, one's beauty, little by little; one is feared like a beast of prey, scorned like a pariah, surrounded by people who always take more than they give; and one fine day one dies like a dog in a ditch, after having ruined others and ruined one's self.'

'Come, come, madame, be calm,' said Nanine; 'your nerves are a bit upset tonight.'

'This dress worries me,' continued Marguerite, unhooking her bodice; 'give me a dressing-gown. Well, and Prudence?'

'She has not come yet, but I will send her to you, madame, the moment she comes.'

'There's one, now,' Marguerite went on, as she took off her dress and put on a white dressing-gown, 'there's one who knows very well how to find me when she is in want of me, and yet she can't do me a service decently. She knows I am waiting for an answer. She knows how anxious I am, and I am sure she is going about on her own account, without giving a thought to me.'

'Perhaps she had to wait.'

'Let us have some punch.'

'It will do you no good, madame,' said Nanine.

'So much the better. Bring some fruit, too, and a paté or a wing of chicken; something or other, at once, I am hungry.'

Need I tell you the impression which this scene made upon me, or can you not imagine it?

'You are going to have supper with me,' she said to me; 'meanwhile, take a book. I am going into my dressing-room for a moment.'

She lit the candles of a candelabra, opened a door at the foot of the bed, and disappeared.

I began to think over this poor girl's life, and my love for her was mingled with a great pity. I walked to and fro in the room, thinking over things, when Prudence entered.

'Ah, you here?' she said; 'where is Marguerite?'

'In her dressing-room.'

'I will wait. By the way, do you know she thinks you charming?'

'No.'

'She hasn't told you?'

'Not at all.'

'How are you here?'

'I have come to pay her a visit.'

'At midnight?'

'Why not?'

'Joker!'

'She has received me, as a matter of fact, very badly.'

'She will receive you better by and by.'

'Do you think so?'

'I have some good news for her.'

'No harm in that. So she has spoken to you about me?'

'Last night, or rather tonight, when you and your friend went. By the way, what is your friend called? Gaston R., his name is isn't it?'

'Yes,' said I, not without smiling, as I thought of what Gaston had confided to me, and saw that Prudence scarcely even knew his name.

'He is quite nice, that fellow; what does he do?'

'He has twenty-five thousand francs a year.'

'Ah, indeed! Well, to return to you. Marguerite asked me all about you: who you were, what you did, what mistresses you had had; in short, everything that one could ask about a man of your age. I told her all I knew, and added that you were a charming young man. That's all.'

'Thanks. Now tell me what it was she wanted to say to you last night.'

'Nothing at all. It was only to get rid of the count; but I have really something to see her about today, and I am bringing her an answer now.'

At this moment Marguerite reappeared from her dressing-room wearing a coquettish little night-cap with bunches of yellow ribbons, technically know as 'cabbages'. She looked ravishing. She had satin slippers on her bare feet, and was in the act of polishing her nails.

'Well,' she said, seeing Prudence, 'have you seen the duke?'

'Yes, indeed.'

'And what did he say to you?'

'He gave me —'

'How much?'

'Six thousand.'

'Have you got it?'

'Yes.'

'Did he seem put out?'

'No.'

'Poor man!'

This 'Poor man!' was said in a tone impossible to render. Marguerite took the six notes of a thousand francs.

'It was quite time,' she said. 'My dear Prudence, are you in want of any money?'

'You know, my child, it is the 15th in a couple of days, so if you could lend me three or four hundred francs, you would do me a real service.'

'Send over tomorrow; it is too late to get change now.'

'Don't forget.'

'No fear. Will you have supper with us?'

'No, Charles is waiting for me.'

'You are still devoted to him?'

'Crazy, my dear! I will see you tomorrow. Good-bye Armand.'

Mme. Duvernoy went out.

Marguerite opened the drawer of a side-table and threw the bank-notes into it.

'Will you permit me to get into bed?' she said with a smile, as she moved toward the bed.

'Not only permit, but I beg of you.'

She turned back the covering and got into bed.

'Now', said she, 'come and sit down by me, and let's have a talk.'

Prudence was right; the answer that she had brought to Marguerite had put her into a good humour.

'Will you forgive me my bad temper tonight?' she said, taking my hand.

'I am ready to forgive you as often as you like.'

'And you love me?'

'Madly.'

'In spite of my bad disposition?'

'In spite of all.'

'You swear it?'

'Yes,' I said in a whisper.

Nanine entered, carrying plates, a cold chicken, a bottle of claret, and some strawberries.

'I haven't had any punch made,' said Nanine; 'claret is better for you. Isn't it sir?'

'Certainly,' I replied, still under the excitement of Marguerite's last words, my eyes fixed ardently upon her.

'Good,' said she, 'put it all on the little table, and draw it up to the bed; we will help ourselves. This is the third night you have sat up, and you must be in want of sleep. Go to bed. I don't want anything more.'

'Shall I lock the door?'

'I should think so! And above all, tell them not to admit anybody before midday.'

CHAPTER XII

At five o'clock in the morning, as the light began to appear through the curtains, Marguerite said to me: 'Forgive me if I send you away; but I must. The duke comes every morning; they will tell him, when he comes, that I am asleep, and perhaps he will wait until I wake.'

I took Marguerite's head in my hands; her loosened hair streamed about her; I gave her a last kiss, saying:

'When shall I see you again?'

'Listen,' she said; 'take the little gilt key on the mantelpiece, open that door; bring me back the key and go. In the course of the day you shall have a letter, and my orders, for you know you are to obey blindly.'

'Yes; but if I should already ask for something?'

'What?'

'Let me have that key.'

'What you ask is a thing I have never done for any one.'

'Well, do it for me, for I swear to you that I don't love you as the others have loved you.'

'Well, keep it; but it depends on me to make it useless to you, after all.'

'How?'

'There are bolts on the door.'

'Wretch!'

'I will have them taken off.'

'You love, then, a little?'

'I don't know how it is, but it seems to me as if I do! Now, go; I can't keep my eyes open.'

I held her in my arms for a few seconds and then went.

The streets were empty, the great city was still asleep, a sweet freshness circulated in the streets that a few hours later would be filled with the noise of men. It seemed to me as if this sleeping city belonged to me; I searched my memory for the names of those whose happiness I had once envied; and I could not recall one without finding myself the happier.

To be loved by a pure young girl, to be the first to reveal to her the strange mystery of love, is indeed a great happiness, but it is the simplest thing in the world. To take captive a heart which has had no experience of attack, is to enter an unfortified and ungarrisoned city. Education, family feeling, the sense of duty, the family, are strong sentinels, but there are no sentinels so vigilant as not to be deceived by a girl of sixteen to whom nature, by the voice of the man she loves gives the first counsels of love, all the more ardent because they seem so pure.

The more a girl believes in goodness, the more easily will she give way, if not to her lover, at least to love, for being without mistrust she is without force, and to win her love is a triumph that can be gained by any young man of five-and-twenty. See how young girls are watched and guarded! The walls of convents are not high enough, mothers have no locks strong enough, religion has no duties constant enough to shut these charming birds in their cages, cages not even strewn with flowers. Then how surely must they desire the world which is hidden from them, how surely must they find it tempting, how surely must they listen to the first voice which comes to tell its secrets through their bars, and bless the hand that is the first to raise a corner of the mysterious veil!

But to be really loved by a courtesan: that is a victory of infinitely greater difficulty. With them the body has worn out the soul, the senses have burned up the heart, dissipation has blunted the feelings. They have long known the words that we say to them, the means we use; they have sold the love that they inspire. They love by profession, and not by instinct. They are guarded better by their calculations than a virgin by her mother and her convent; and they have invented the word caprice for that unbartered love which they allow themselves from time to time, for a rest, for an excuse, for a consolation, like usurers, who cheat a thousand, and think they have bought their own redemption by once lending a sovereign to a poor devil who is dying of hunger without asking for interest or a receipt.

Then, when God allows love to a courtesan, that love, which at first seems like a pardon, becomes for her almost always a punishment. There is no absolution without penitence. When a creature who has all her past to reproach herself with is taken all at once by a profound, sincere, irresistible love, of which she had never felt herself capable; when she has confessed her love, how absolutely the man whom she loves dominates her! How strong he feels with his cruel right to say: You do no more for love than you have done for money. They know not what proof to give. A child, says the fable, having often amused himself by crying 'Help! a wolf!' in order to disturb the labourers in the field, was one day devoured by a wolf, because those whom he had so often deceived no longer believed in his cries for help. It is the same with these unhappy women when they love seriously. They have lied so often that no one will believe them, and in the midst of their remorse they are devoured by their love. Hence those great devotions, those austere retreats from the world, of which some of them have given an example.

But when the man who inspires this redeeming love is great enough in soul to receive it without remembering the past, when he gives himself up to it, when, in short, he loves as he is loved, this man drains at one draught all earthly emotions, and after such a love his heart will be closed to every other.

I did not make these reflections on the morning when I returned home. They could but have been the presentiment of what was to happen to me, and, despite my love for Marguerite, I did not foresee such consequences. I make these reflections today. Now that all is irrevocably ended, they arise naturally out of what has taken place.

But to return to the first day of my *liaison*. When I reached home I was in a state of mad gaiety. As I thought of how the barriers which my imagination had placed between Marguerite and myself had disappeared, of how she was now mine; of the place I now had in her thoughts, of the key to her room which I had in my pocket, and of my right to use this key, I was satisfied with life, proud of myself, and I loved God because He had let such things be.

One day a young man is passing in the street, he brushes against a woman, looks at her, turns, goes on his way. He does not know the woman, and she has pleasures, griefs, loves, in which he has no part. He does not exist for her, and perhaps, if he spoke to her, she would only laugh at him, as Marguerite had laughed at me. Weeks, months, years pass, and all at once, when they have each followed their fate along a different path the logic of chance brings them face to face. The woman becomes the man's mistress and loves him. How? Why? Their two existences are henceforth one; they have scarcely begun to know one another when it seems as if they had known one another always, and all that had gone before is wiped out from the memory of the two lovers. It is curious, one must admit.

As for me, I no longer remembered how I had loved before that night. My whole being was exalted into joy at the memory of the words we had exchanged during that first night. Either Marguerite was very clever in deception, or she had conceived for me one of those sudden passions which are revealed in the first kiss, and which die, often enough, as suddenly as they were born.

The more I reflected the more I said to myself that Marguerite had no reason for feigning a love which she did not feel, and I said to myself also that women have two ways of loving, one of which may arise from the other: they love with the heart or with the senses. Often a woman takes a lover in obedience to the mere will of the senses, and learns without expecting it the mystery of immaterial love, and lives henceforth only through her heart; often a girl who has sought in marriage only the union of two pure affections receives the sudden revelation of physical love, that energetic conclusion of the purest impressions of the soul.

In the midst of these thoughts I fell asleep; I was awakened by a letter from Marguerite containing these words:

'Here are my orders: Tonight at the Vaudeville.
'Come during the third *entr'acte*.

'M.G.'

I put the letter into a drawer, so that I might always have it at hand in case I doubted its reality, as I did from time to time.

She did not tell me to come to see her during the day, and I dared not go; but I had so great a desire to see her before the evening that I went to the Champs-Élysées, where I again saw her pass and repass, as I had on the previous day.

At seven o'clock I was at the Vaudeville. Never had I gone to a theatre so early. The boxes filled one after another. Only one remained empty, the stage box, on which my eyes had been almost constantly fixed, open, and Marguerite appeared. She came to the front at once, looked around the stalls, saw me, and thanked me with a look.

That night she was marvellously beautiful. Was I the cause of this coquetry? Did she love me enough to believe that the more beautiful she looked the happier I should be? I did not know, but if that had been her intention she certainly succeeded, for when she appeared all heads turned, and the actor who was then on the stage looked to see who had produced such an effect on the audience by her mere presence there.

And I had the key of this woman's room, and in three or four hours she would again be mine!

People blame those who let themselves be ruined by actresses and kept women; what astonishes me is that twenty times greater follies are not committed for them. One must have lived that life, as I have, to know how much the little vanities which they afford their lovers every day help to fasten deeper into the heart, since we have no other word for it, the love which he has for them.

Prudence next took her place in the box, and a man whom I recognized as the Comte de G., seated himself at the back. As I saw him, a cold shiver went through my heart.

Doubtless Marguerite perceived the impression made on me by the presence of this man, for she smiled to me again, and turning her back to the count, appeared to be very attentive to the play. At the third *entr'acte* she turned and said two words: the count left the box, and Marguerite beckoned to me to come to her.

'Good-evening,' she said as I entered, holding out her hand.

'Good-evening,' I replied to both Marguerite and Prudence.

'Sit down.'

'But I am taking some one's place. Isn't the Comte de G. coming back?'

'Yes; I sent him to fetch some sweets, so that we could talk by ourselves for a moment. Mme. Duvernoy is in the secret.'

'Yes, my children,' said she; 'have no fear. I shall say nothing.'

'What is the matter with you tonight?' said Marguerite, rising and coming to the back of the box and kissing me on the forehead.

'I am not very well.'

'You should go to bed,' she replied, with that ironical air which went so well with her delicate and witty face.

'Where?'

'At home.'

'You know that I shouldn't be able to sleep there.'

'Well, then, it won't do for you to come and be pettish here because you have seen a man in my box.'

'It is not for that reason.'

'Yes, it is. I know; and you are wrong, so let us say no more about it. You will go back with Prudence after the theatre, and you will stay there till I call. Do you understand?'

'Yes.'

How could I disobey?

'You still love me?'

'Can you ask?'

'You have thought of me?'

'All day long.'

'Do you know that I am really afraid that I shall get very fond of you? Ask Prudence.'

'Ah,' said she, 'it is amazing!'

'Now, you must go back to your seat. The count will be coming back, and there is nothing to be gained by his finding you here.'

'Why?'

'Because you don't like seeing him.'

'No; only if you had told me that you wanted to come to the Vaudeville tonight I could have got this box for you as well as he.'

'Unfortunately, he got it for me without my asking him, and he asked me to go with him; you know well enough that I couldn't refuse. All I could do was to write and tell you where I was going, so that you could see me, and because I wanted to see you myself; but since this is the way you thanked me, I shall profit by the lesson.'

'I was wrong; forgive me.'

'Well and good; and now go back nicely to your place, and, above all, no more jealousy.'

She kissed me again, and I left the box. In the passage I met the count coming back. I returned to my seat.

After all, the presence of M. de G. in Marguerite's box was the most natural thing in the world. He had been her lover, he sent her a box, he accompanied her to the theatre; it was all quite natural, and if I was to have a mistress like Marguerite I should have to get used to her ways.

None the less, I was very unhappy the rest of the evening, and went away very sadly after having seen Prudence, the count, and Marguerite get into the carriage, which was waiting for them at the door.

However, a quarter of an hour later I was at Prudence's. She had only just got in.

CHAPTER XIII

'You have come almost as quickly as we,' said Prudence.

'Yes.' I answered mechanically. 'Where is Marguerite?'

'At home.'

'Alone?'

'With M. de G.'

I walked to and fro in the room.

'Well, what is the matter?'

'Do you think it amuses me to wait here till M. de G. leaves Marguerite's?'

'How unreasonable you are! Don't you see that Marguerite can't turn the count out of doors? M. de G. has been with her for a long time; he has always given her a lot of money; he still does. Marguerite spends more than a hundred thousand francs a year; she has heaps of debts. The duke gives her all that she asks for, but she does not always venture to ask him for all that she is in want of. It would never do for her to quarrel with the count, who is worth to her at least ten thousand francs a year. Marguerite is very fond of you, my dear fellow, but your *liaison* with her, in her interests and in yours, ought not to be serious. You with your seven or eight thousand francs a year, what could you do toward supplying all the luxuries which a girl like that is in need of? It would not be enough to keep her carriage. Take Marguerite for what she is, for a good, bright, pretty girl; be her lover for a month, two months; give her flowers, sweets, boxes at the theatre; but don't get any other ideas into your head, and don't make absurd scenes of jealousy. You know whom you have to do with; Marguerite isn't a saint. She likes you, you are very fond of her; let the rest alone. You amaze me when I see you so touchy; you have the most charming mistress in Paris. She receives you in the greatest style, she is covered with diamonds, she needn't cost you a penny, unless you like, and you are not satisfied. My dear fellow, you ask too much!'

'You are right, but I can't help it; the idea that that man is her lover hurts me horribly.'

'In the first place,' replied Prudence; 'is he still her lover? He is a man who is useful to her, nothing more. She has closed her doors to him for two days; he came this morning – she could not but accept the box and let him accompany her. He saw her home; he has gone in for a moment, he is not staying, because you are waiting here. All that, it seems to me, is quite natural. Besides, you don't mind the duke.'

'Yes; but he is an old man, and I am sure that Marguerite is not his mistress. Then, it is all very well to accept one *liaison*, but not two. Such easiness in the matter is very like calculation, and puts the man who consents to it, even out of love, very much in the category of those who, in a lower stage of society, make a trade of their connivance, and a profit of their trade.'

'Ah, my dear fellow, how old-fashioned you are! How many of the richest and most fashionable men of the best families I have seen quite ready to do what I advise you to do, and without an effort, without shame, without remorse! Why, one sees it every day. How do you suppose the kept women in Paris could live in the style they do, if they had not three or four lovers at once? No single fortune, however large, could suffice for the expenses of a woman like Marguerite. A fortune of five hundred thousand francs a year is, in France, an enormous fortune; well, my dear friend, five hundred thousand francs a year would still be too little, and for this reason: a man with such an income has a large house, horses, servants, carriages; he shoots, has friends, often he is married, he has children, he races, gambles, travels, and what not. All these habits are so much a part of his position that he can not forego them without appearing to have lost all his money, and without causing scandal. Taking it all around, with five hundred thousand francs in the year he can not give a woman more than forty or fifty thousand francs in the year, and that is already a good deal. Well, other lovers make up for the rest of her expenses. With Marguerite, it is still more convenient; she has chanced by a miracle on an old man worth ten millions, whose wife and daughter are dead; who has only some nephews, themselves rich, and who gives her all she wants without asking anything in return. But she cannot ask him for more than seventy thousand francs a year; and I am sure that if she did ask for more, despite his wealth and the affection he has for her, he would not give it to her.

'All the young men of twenty or thirty thousand francs a year in Paris, that is to say, men who have only just enough to live on in the society in which they mix, know perfectly well, when they are the lovers of a woman like Marguerite, that she could not so much as pay for the rooms she lives in and the servants who wait upon her with what they give her. They do not say to her that they know it; they pretend not to see anything, and when they have had enough of it they go their way. If they have the vanity to wish to pay for everything they get ruined, like the fools they are, and go and get killed in Africa, after leaving a hundred thousand francs of debt in Paris. Do you think a woman is grateful to them for it? Far from it. She declares that she has sacrificed her position for them, and that while she was with them she was losing money. These details seem to you shocking? Well, they are true. You are a very nice fellow; I like you very much. I have lived with these women for twenty years; I know what they are worth, and I don't want to see you take the caprice that a pretty girl has for you too seriously.

'Then, besides that,' continued Prudence; 'admit that Marguerite loves you enough to give up the count or the duke, in case one of them were to discover your *liaison* and to tell her to choose between him and you, the sacrifice that she would make for you would be enormous, you can not deny it. What equal sacrifice could you make for her, on your part, and when you had got tired of her, what could you do to make up for what you had taken from her? Nothing. You would have cut her off from the world in which her fortune and her future were to be found; she would have given you her best years, and she would be forgotten. Either you would be an ordinary man, and casting her past in her teeth, you would leave her, telling her that you were only doing like her other lovers, and you would abandon her to certain misery; or you would be an honest man, and, feeling bound to keep her by you, you would bring inevitable trouble upon yourself, for a *liaison* which is excusable in a young man, is no longer excusable in a man of middle age. It becomes an obstacle to everything; it allows neither family nor ambition, man's second and last loves. Believe me, then, my friend, take things for what they are worth, and do not give a kept woman the right to call herself your creditor, no matter in what.'

It was well argued, with a logic of which I should have thought Prudence incapable. I had nothing to reply, except that she was right; I took her hand and thanked her for her counsels.

'Come, come,' said she, 'put these foolish theories to flight and laugh over them. Life is pleasant my dear fellow; it all depends on the colour of the glass through which one sees it. Ask your friend Gaston; there's a man who seems to me to understand love as I understand it. All that you need think of, unless you are quite a fool, is that close by there is a beautiful girl who is waiting impatiently for the man who is with her to go, thinking of you, keeping the whole night for you, and who loves you, I am certain. Now, come to the window with me, and let us watch for the count to go; he won't be long in leaving the coast clear.'

Prudence opened the window, and we leaned side by side over the balcony. She watched the few passers, I reflected. All that she had said buzzed in my head, and I could not help feeling that she was right; but the genuine love which I had for Marguerite had some difficulty in accommodating itself to such a belief. I sighed from time to time, at which Prudence turned, and shrugged her shoulders like a physician who has given up his patient.

'How one realizes the shortness of life,' I said to myself, 'by the rapidity of sensations! I have only known Marguerite for two days, she has only been my mistress since yesterday, and she has already so completely absorbed my thoughts, my heart, and my life that the visit of the Comte de G. is a misfortune to me.'

At last the count came out, got into his carriage and disappeared. Prudence closed the window. At the same instant Marguerite called to us;

'Come at once,' she said; 'they are laying the table, and we'll have supper.'

When I entered, Marguerite ran to me, threw her arms around my neck and kissed me with all her might.

'Are we still sulky?' she said to me.

'No, it is all over,' replied Prudence. 'I have given him a talking to, and he has promised to be reasonable.'

'Well and good.'

In spite of myself I glanced at the bed; it was not unmade. As for Marguerite, she was already in her white dressing-gown. We sat down to table.

Charm, sweetness, spontaneity, Marguerite had them all, and I was forced from time to time to admit that I had no right to ask her anything else; that many people would be very happy to be in my place; and that, like Virgil's shepherd, I had only to enjoy the pleasures that a god, or rather a goddess, set before me.

I tried to put in practice the theories of Prudence, and to be as gay as my two companions; but what was natural in them was on my part an effort, and the nervous laughter, whose source they did not detect, was nearer to tears than to mirth.

At last the supper was over and I was alone with Marguerite. She sat down as usual on the hearth-rug before the fire and gazed sadly into the flames. What was she thinking of? I know not. As for me, I looked at her with a mingling of love and terror, as I thought of all that I was ready to suffer for her sake.

'Do you know what I am thinking of?'

'No.'

'Of a plan that has come into my head.'

'And what is this plan?'

'I can't tell you yet, but I can tell you what the result would be. The result would be that in a month I should be free, I should have no more debts, and we could go and spend the summer in the country.'

'And you can't tell me by what means?'

'No, only love me as I love you, and all will succeed.'

'And have you made this plan all by yourself?'

'Yes.'

'And shall you carry it out all by yourself?'

'I alone shall have the trouble of it,' said Marguerite, with a smile which I shall never forget, 'but we shall both partake its benefits.'

I could not help flushing at the word benefits; I thought of
Manon Lescaut squandering with Desgrieux the money of M.
de B.

I replied in a hard voice, rising from my seat:

'You must permit me, my dear Marguerite, to share only
the benefits of those enterprises which I have conceived and
carried out myself.'

'What does that mean?'

'It means that I have a strong suspicion that M. de G. is to be
your associate in this pretty plan, of which I can accept neither
the cost nor the benefits.'

'What a child you are! I thought you loved me. I was
mistaken; all right.'

She rose, opened the piano and began to play the Invitation
à la Valse, as far as the famous passage in the major which
always stopped her. Was it through force of habit, or was it to
remind me of the day when we first met? All I know is that the
melody brought back the recollection, and, coming up to her,
I took her head between my hands and kissed her.

'You forgive me?' I said.

'You see I do,' she answered; 'but observe that we are only
at our second day, and already I have had to forgive you
something. Is this how you keep your promise of blind
obedience?'

'What can I do, Marguerite? I love you too much and I am
jealous of the least of your thoughts. What you proposed to
me just now made me frantic with delight, but the mystery in
its carrying out hurts me dreadfully.'

'Come, let us reason it out,' she said, taking both my hands
and looking at me with a charming smile which it was
impossible to resist. 'You love me, do you not? And would
gladly spend two or three months alone with me in the
country? I too should be glad of this *solitude à deux*, and not
only glad of it, but my health requires it. I can not leave Paris
for such a length of time without putting my affairs in order,
and the affairs of a woman like me are always in great
confusion; well, I have found a way to reconcile everything,
my money affairs and my love for you; yes, for you, don't
laugh; I am silly enough to love you! And here you are taking
lordly airs and talking big words. Child, thrice child, only

remember that I love you, and don't let anything disturb you. Now, it is agreed?'

'I agree to all you wish, as you know.'

'Then, in less than a month's time we shall be in some village, walking by the river side, and drinking milk. Does it seem strange that Marguerite Gautier should speak to you like that? The fact is, my friend, that when this Paris life, which seems to make me so happy, doesn't burn me, it wearies me, and then I have sudden aspirations toward a calmer existence which might recall my childhood. One has always had a child-hood, whatever one becomes. Don't be alarmed; I am not going to tell you that I am the daughter of a colonel on half-pay, and that I was brought up at Saint-Denis. I am a poor country-girl, and six years ago I could not write my own name. You are relieved, aren't you? Why is it you are the first whom I have ever asked to share the joy of this desire of mine? I suppose because I feel that you love me for myself, and not for yourself, while all the others have only loved me for themselves.

'I have often been in the country, but never as I should like to go there. I count on you for this easy happiness; do not be un-kind, let me have it. Say this to yourself "She will never live to be old, and I should some day be sorry for not having done for her the first thing she asked of me, such an easy thing to do!"'

What could I reply to such words, especially with the memory of a first night of love, and in the expectation of a second?

An hour later I held Marguerite in my arms, and, if she had asked me to commit a crime, I would have obeyed her.

At six in the morning I left her, and before leaving her I said: 'Till tonight?'

She kissed me more warmly that ever, but said nothing.

During the day I received a note containing these words:

'DEAR CHILD: I am not very well, and the doctor has ordered quiet. I shall go to bed early tonight and shall not see you. But, to make up, I shall expect you tomorrow at twelve. I love you.'

My first thought was: She is deceiving me!

A cold sweat broke out on my forehead, for I already loved this woman too much not to be overwhelmed with suspicion.

And yet, I was bound to expect such a thing almost any day with Marguerite, and it had happened to me often enough with my other mistresses, without my taking much notice of it. What was the meaning of the hold which this woman had taken upon my life?

Then it occurred to me, since I had the key, to go and see her as usual. In this way I should soon know the truth, and if I found a man there I would strike him in the face.

Meanwhile I went to the Champs-Élysées. I waited there four hours. She did not appear. At night I went into all the theatres where she was accustomed to go. She was in none of them.

At eleven o'clock, I went to the Rue d'Antin. There was no light in Marguerite's windows. All the same, I rang. The porter asked me where I was going.

'To Mlle. Gautier's,' I said.

'She has not come in.'

'I will go up and wait for her.'

'There is no one there.'

Evidently I could get in, since I had the key, but, fearing foolish scandal, I went away. Only I did not return home; I could not leave the street, and I never took my eyes off Marguerite's house. It seemed to me that there was still something to be found out, or at least that my suspicions were about to be confirmed.

About midight a carriage that I knew well stopped before No. 9. The Comte de G. got down and entered the house, after sending away the carriage. For a moment I hoped that the same answer would be given to him as to me, and that I should see him come out; but at four o'clock in the morning I was still awaiting him.

I have suffered deeply during the last three weeks, but that is nothing, I think, in comparison with what I suffered that night.

CHAPTER XIV

When I reached home I began to cry like a child. There is no man to whom a woman has been unfaithful, once at least, who will not know what I suffered.

I said to myself, under the weight of these feverish resolutions which one always feels as if one had the force to carry out, that I must break with my amour at once, and I waited impatiently for daylight in order to set out forthwith to rejoin my father and my sister, of whose love at least I was certain, and certain that that love would never be betrayed.

However, I did not wish to go away without letting Marguerite know why I went. Only a man who really cares no more for his mistress leaves her without writing to her. I made and remade twenty letters in my head. I had had to do with a woman like all other women of the kind. I had been poetizing too much. She had treated me like a schoolboy, she had used in deceiving me a trick which was insultingly simple. My self-esteem got the upper hand. I must leave this woman without giving her the satisfaction of knowing that she had made me suffer, and this is what I wrote to her in my most elegant handwriting and with tears of rage and sorrow in my eyes:

'MY DEAR MARGUERITE: I hope that your indisposition yesterday was not serious. I came at eleven at night, to ask for you, and was told that you had not come in. M. de G. was more fortunate, for he presented himself shortly afterward, and at four in the morning he had not left.

'Forgive me for the few tedious hours that I have given you, and be assured that I shall never forget the happy moments which I owe to you.

'I should have called today to ask after you, but I intend going back to my father's.

'Good-bye, my dear Marguerite. I am not rich enough to love you as I would, nor poor enough to love you as you would. Let us then forget, you a name which must be indifferent enough to you, I a happiness which has become impossible.

'I send back your key, which I have never used, and which might be useful to you if you are often ill as you were yesterday.'

As you will see, I was unable to end my letter without a touch of impertinent irony, which proved how much in love I still was.

I read and reread this letter ten times over; then the thought of the pain it would give to Marguerite calmed me a little. I tried to persuade myself of the feeling which it professed; and when my servant came to my room at eight o'clock, I gave it to him and told him to take it at once.

'Shall I wait for an answer?' asked Joseph (my servant, like all servants, was called Joseph).

'If they ask whether there is a reply, you will say that you don't know, and wait.'

I buoyed myself up with the hope that she would reply. Poor, feeble creatures that we are! All the time that my servant was away I was in a state of extreme agitation. At one moment I would recall how Marguerite had given herself to me, and ask myself by what right I wrote her an impertinent letter, when she could reply that it was not M. de G. who supplanted me, but I who had supplanted M. de G.: a mode of reasoning which permits many women to have many lovers. At another moment I would recall her promises, and endeavour to convince myself that my letter was only too gentle, and that there were not expressions forcible enough to punish a woman who laughed at a love like mine. Then I said to myself that I should have done better not to have written to her, but to have gone to see her, and that then I should have had the pleasure of seeing the tears that she would shed. Finally, I asked myself what she would reply to me; already prepared to believe whatever excuse she made.

Joseph returned.

'Well?' I said to him.

'Sir', said he, 'madame was not up, and still asleep, but as soon as she rings the letter will be taken to her, and if there is any reply it will be sent.'

She was asleep!

Twenty times I was on the point of sending to get the letter back, but every time I said to myself: 'Perhaps she will have got it already, and it would look as if I have repented of sending it.'

As the hour at which it seemed likely that she would reply came nearer, I regretted more and more that I had written. The clock struck ten, eleven, twelve. At twelve I was on the point of keeping the appointment as if nothing had happened. In the end I could see no way out of the circle of fire which closed upon me.

Then I began to believe, with the superstition which people have when they are waiting, that if I went out for a little while, I should find an answer when I got back. I went out under the pretext of going to lunch.

Instead of lunching at the Café Foy, at the corner of the Boulevard, as I usually did, I preferred to go to the Palais Royal and so pass through the Rue d'Antin. Every time that I saw a woman at a distance, I fancied that it was Nanine bringing me an answer. I passed through the Rue d'Antin without even coming across a *commissionaire*. I went to Véry's in the Palais Royal. The waiter gave me something to eat, or rather served up to me whatever he liked, for I ate nothing. In spite of myself, my eyes were constantly fixed on the clock. I returned home, certain that I should find a letter from Marguerite.

The porter had received nothing, but I still hoped in my servant. He had seen no one since I went out.

If Marguerite had been going to answer me she would have answered long before.

Then I began to regret the terms of my letter; I should have said absolutely nothing, and that would undoubtedly have aroused her suspicions, for, finding that I did not keep my appointment, she would have inquired the reason of my absence, and only then I should have given it to her. Thus, she would have had to exculpate herself. I already realized that I should have believed whatever reasons she had given me, and anything was better than not to see her again.

At last I began to believe that she would come to see me herself; but hour followed hour, and she did not come.

Decidedly Marguerite was not like other women, for there are few who would have received such a letter as I had just written without answering it at all.

At five, I hastened to the Champs-Élysées. 'If I meet her,' I thought, 'I will put on an indifferent air, and she will be convinced that I no longer think about her.'

As I turned the corner of the Rue Royale, I saw her pass in her carriage. The meeting was so sudden that I turned pale. I do not know if she saw my emotion; as for me, I was so agitated that I saw nothing but the carriage.

I did not go any farther in the direction of the Champs-Élysées. I looked at the advertisements of the theatres, for I had still a chance of seeing her. There was a first night at the Palais Royal. Marguerite was sure to be there. I was at the theatre by seven. The boxes filled one after another, but Marguerite was not there. I left the Palais Royal and went to all the theatres where she was most often to be seen: to the Vaudeville, the Variétés, the Opéra Comique. She was nowhere.

Either my letter had troubled her too much for her to care to go to the theatre, or she feared to come across me, and so wished to avoid an explanation. So my vanity was whispering to me on the boulevards, when I met Gaston, who asked me where I had been.

'At the Palais Royal.'

'And I at the Opéra,' said he; 'I expected to see you there.'

'Why?'

'Because Marguerite was there.'

'Ah, she was there?'

'Yes.'

'Alone?'

'No; with another woman.'

'That all?'

'The Comte de G. came to her box for an instant; but she went off with the duke. I expected to see you every moment, for there was a stall at my side which remained empty the whole evening, and I was sure you had taken it.'

'But why should I go where Marguerite goes?'

'Because you are her lover, surely!'

'Who told you that?'

'Prudence, whom I met yesterday. I give you my congratulations, my dear fellow; she is a charming mistress, and it isn't everyone who has the chance. Stick to her; she will do you credit.'

These simple reflections of Gaston showed me how absurd had been my susceptibilities. If I had only met him the night before and he had spoken to me like that, I should certainly not have written the foolish letter which I had written.

I was on the point of calling on Prudence, and of sending her to tell Marguerite that I wanted to speak to her; but I feared that she would revenge herself on me by saying that she could not see me, and I returned home, after passing through the Rue d'Antin. Again I asked my porter if there was a letter for me. Nothing! She is waiting to see if I shall take some fresh step, and if I retract my letter of today, I said to myself as I went to bed; but, seeing that I do not write, she will write to me tomorrow.

That night, more than ever, I reproached myself for what I had done. I was alone, unable to sleep, devoured by restlessness and jealousy, when by simply letting things take their natural course I should have been with Marguerite, hearing the delicious words which I had heard only twice, and which made my ears burn in my solitude.

The most frightful part of the situation was that my judgment was against me; as a matter of fact everything went to prove that Marguerite loved me. First, her proposal to spend the summer with me in the country, then the certainty there was no reason why she should be my mistress, since my income was insufficient for her needs and even for her caprices. There could not then have been on her part anything but the hope of finding in me a sincere affection, able to give her rest from the mercenary loves in whose midst she lived; and on the very second day I had destroyed this hope, and paid by impertinent irony for the love which I had accepted during two nights. What I had done was therefore not merely ridiculous, it was indelicate. I had not even paid the woman, that I might have some right to find fault with her; withdrawing after two days, was I not like a parasite of love, afraid of having to pay the bill of the banquet? What! I had only known Marguerite for thirty-six hours; I had been her lover for only twenty-four; and instead of being too happy that she should grant me all that she did, I wanted to have her all to myself, and to make her sever at one stroke all her past relations which were the revenue of the future. What had I to reproach in her? Nothing. She had written to say she was unwell, when she might have said to me quite crudely, with the hideous frankness of certain women, that she had to see a lover; and, instead of believing her letter, instead of going to any street in Paris except the Rue d'Antin, instead of spending the evening with my friends, and presenting myself next day at the appointed hour, I was acting the Othello, spying upon her, and thinking to punish her by seeing her no more. But, on the contrary, she ought to be enchanted at this separation. She ought to find me supremely foolish, and her silence was not even that of rancour; it was contempt.

I might have made Marguerite a present which would leave no doubt as to my generosity and permit me to feel properly quits of her, as of a kept woman, but I should have felt that I was offending by the least appearance of trafficking, if not the love which she had for me, at all events the love which I had for her, and since this love was so pure that it could admit no division, it could not pay by a present, however generous, the happiness that it had received, however short that happiness had been.

That is what I said to myself all night long, and what I was every moment prepared to go and say to Marguerite. When the day dawned I was still sleepless. I was in a fever. I could think of nothing but Marguerite.

As you can imagine, it was time to take a decided step, and finish either with the woman or with one's scruples, if that is, she would still be willing to see me. But you know well, one is always slow in taking a decided step; so, unable to remain within doors and not daring to call on Marguerite, I made one attempt in her direction, an attempt that I could always look upon as a mere chance if it succeeded.

It was nine o'clock, and I went at once to call upon Prudence, who asked to what she owed this early visit. I dared not tell her frankly what brought me. I replied that I had gone out early in order to reserve a place in the coach for C., where my father lived.

'You are fortunate,' she said, 'in being able to get away from Paris in this fine weather.'

I looked at Prudence, asking myself whether she was laughing at me, but her face was quite serious.

'Shall you go and say good-bye to Marguerite?' she continued, as seriously as before.

'No.'

'You are quite right.'

'You think so?'

'Naturally. Since you have broken with her, why should you see her again?'

'You know it is broken off?'

'She showed me your letter.'

'What did she say about it?'

'She said:"My dear Prudence, your protégé is not polite; one thinks such letters, one does not write them."'

'In what tone did she say that?'

'Laughingly, and she added:"He has had supper with me twice, and hasn't even called."'

That, then, was the effect produced by my letter and my jealousy. I was cruelly humiliated in the vanity of my affection.

'What did she do last night?'

'She went to the opera.'

'I know. And afterward?'

'She had supper at home.'

'Alone?'

'With the Comte de G., I believe.'

So my breaking with her had not changed one of her habits. It is for such reasons as this that certain people say to you: Don't have anything more to do with that woman; she cares nothing about you.

'Well, I am very glad to find that Margerite does not put herself out for me,' I said with a forced smile.

'She has very good reason not to. You have done what you were bound to do. You have been more reasonable than she, for she was really in love with you; she did nothing but talk of you. I don't know what she would not have been capable of doing.'

'Why hasn't she answered me, if she was in love with me?'

'Because she realizes she was mistaken in letting herself love you. Women sometimes allow you to be unfaithful to their love; they never allow you to wound their self-esteem; and one always wounds the self-esteem of a woman when, two days after one has become her lover, one leaves her, no matter for what reason. I know Marguerite; she would die sooner than reply.'

'What can I do, then.'

'Nothing. She will forget you, you will forget her, and neither will have any reproach to make against the other.'

'But if I write and ask her forgiveness?'

'Don't do that, for she would forgive you.'

I could have thrown my arms round Prudence's neck.

A quarter of an hour later I was once more in my own quarters, and I wrote to Marguerite:

'Some one, who repents of a letter that he wrote yesterday and who will leave Paris tomorrow if you do not forgive him, wishes to know at what hour he might lay his repentance at your feet.

'When can he find you alone? for, you know, confessions must be made without witnesses.'

I folded this kind of madrigal in prose, and sent it by Joseph, who handed it to Marguerite herself; she replied that she would send the answer later.

I only went out to have a hasty dinner, and at eleven in the evening no reply had come. I made up my mind to endure it no longer, and to set out next day. In consequence of this resolution, and convinced that I should not sleep if I went to bed, I began to pack my things.

CHAPTER XV

It was hardly an hour after Joseph and I had begun preparing for my departure, when there was a violent ring at the door.

'Shall I go to the door?' said Joseph.

'Go,' I said, asking myself who it could be at such an hour, and not daring to believe it was Marguerite.

'Sir,' said Joseph coming back to me, 'it is two ladies.'

'It is we, Armand,' cried a voice that I recognized as that of Prudence.

I came out of my room. Prudence was standing looking around the place; Marguerite, seated on the sofa, was meditating. I went to her, knelt down, took her two hands, and, deeply moved, said to her, 'Pardon.'

She kissed me on the forehead, and said:

'This is the third time that I have forgiven you.'

'I should have gone away tomorrow.'

'How can my visit change your plans? I have not come to hinder you from leaving Paris. I have come because I had no time to answer you during the day, and I did not wish to let you think that I was angry with you. Prudence didn't want me to come; she said that I might be in the way.'

'You in the way, Marguerite! But how?'

'Well, you might have had a woman here,' said Prudence, 'and it would hardly have been amusing for her to see two more arrive.'

During this remark Marguerite looked at me attentively.

'My dear Prudence,' I answered, 'you do not know what you are saying.'

'What a nice place you've got!' Prudence went on. 'May we see the bedroom?'

'Yes.'

Prudence went into the bedroom, not so much as to see it as to make up for the foolish thing which she had just said, and to leave Marguerite and me alone.

'Why did you bring Prudence?' I asked her.

'Because she was at the theatre with me, and because when I leave here I want to have some one to see me home.'

'Could not I do?'

'Yes, but, besides not wishing to put you out, I was sure that if you came as far as my door you would want to come up, and as I could not let you, I did not wish to let you go away blaming me for saying "No".'

'And why could you not let me come up?'

'Because I am watched, and the least suspicion might do me the greatest harm.'

'Is that really the only reason?'

'If there were any other, I would tell you; for we are not to have any secrets from one another now.'

'Come, Marguerite, I am not going to take a roundabout way of saying what I really want to say. Honestly, do you care for me a little?'

'A great deal.'

'Then why do you deceive me?'

'My friend, if I were the Duchess So and So, if I had two hundred thousand francs a year, and if I were your mistress and had another lover, you would have the right to ask me; but I am Mlle. Marguerite Gautier, I am forty thousand francs in debt, I have not a penny of my own, and I spend a hundred thousand francs a year. Your question becomes unnecessary and my answer useless.'

'You are right,' I said, letting my head sink on her knees; 'but I love you madly.'

'Well, my friend, you must either love me a little less or understand me a little better. Your letter gave me a great deal of pain. If I had been free, first of all I would not have seen the count the day before yesterday, or, if I had, I should have come and asked your forgiveness as you ask me now, and in future I should have had no other lover but you. I fancied for a moment that I might give myself that happiness for six months; you would not have it; you insisted on knowing the means. Well, good heavens, the means were easy enough to guess! In employing them I was making a greater sacrifice for you than you imagine. I might have said to you, "I want twenty thousand francs"; you were in love with me and you would have found them, at the risk of reproaching me for it later on. I preferred to owe you nothing; you did not understand the scruple, for such it was. Those of us who are like me, when we have any heart at all, we give a meaning and a development to words and things unknown to other women; I repeat, then, that on the part of Marguerite Gautier the means which she used to pay her debts without asking you for the money necessary for it, was a scruple by which you ought to profit, without saying anything. If you had only met me today, you would be too delighted with what I promised you, and you would not question me as to what I did the day before yesterday. We are sometimes obliged to buy the satisfaction of our souls at the expense of our bodies, and we suffer still more, when, afterward, that satisfaction is denied us.'

I listened, and I gazed at Marguerite with admiration. When I thought that this marvellous creature, whose feet I had once longed to kiss, was willing to let me take my place in her thoughts, my part in her life, and that I was not yet content with what she gave me, I asked if man's desire has indeed limits when, satisfied as promptly as mine had been, it reached after something further.

'Truly,' she continued, 'we poor creatures of chance have fantastic desires and inconceivable loves. We give ourselves now for one thing, now for another. There are men who ruin themselves without obtaining the least thing from us; there are others who obtain us for a bouquet of flowers. Our hearts have their caprices; it is their one distraction and their one excuse. I gave myself to you sooner than I ever did to any man, I swear to you; and do you know why? Because when you saw me spitting blood you took my hand; because you wept; because you are the only human being who has ever pitied me. I am going to say a mad thing to you: I once had a little dog who looked at me with a sad look when I coughed; that is the only creaure I ever loved. When he died I cried more than when my mother died. It is true that for twelve years of her life she used to beat me. Well, I loved you all at once, as much as my dog. If men knew what they can have for a tear, they would be better loved and we should be less ruinous to them.

'Your letter undeceived me; it showed me that you lacked the intelligence of the heart; it did you more harm with me than anything you could possibly have done. It was jealousy certainly, but ironical and impertinent jealousy. I was already feeling sad when I received your letter. I was looking forward to seeing you at twelve, to having lunch with you, and wiping out, by seeing you, a thought which was with me incessantly, and which, before I knew you, I had no difficulty in tolerating.

'Then,' continued Marguerite, 'you were the only person before whom it seemed to me, from the first, that I could think and speak freely. All those who come about women like me have an interest in calculating their slightest words, in thinking of the consequences of their most insignificant actions. Naturally we have no friends. We have selfish lovers who spend their fortunes, not on us, as they say, but on their own vanity. For these people we have to be merry when they are merry, well when they want to sup, sceptics like themselves. We are not allowed to have hearts, under penalty of being hooted down and of ruining our credit.

'We no longer belong to ourselves. We are no longer beings, but things. We stand first in their self-esteem, last in their esteem. We have women who call themselves our friends, but they are friends like Prudence, women who were once kept and who have still the costly tastes that their age does not allow them to gratify. Then they become our friends, or rather our guests at table. Their friendship is carried to the point of servility, never to that of disinterestedness. Never do they give you advice which is not lucrative. It means little enough to them that we should have ten lovers extra, as long as they get dresses or a bracelet out of them, and they can drive in our carriage from time to time or come to our box at the theatre. They have our last night's bouquets, and they borrow our shawls. They never render us a service, however slight, without seeing that they are paid twice its value. You yourself saw when Prudence brought me the six thousand francs that I had asked her to get from the duke, how she borrowed five hundred francs, which she will never pay me back, or which she will pay me in hats, which will never be taken out of their boxes.

'We can not, then, have, or rather I can not have more than one possible kind of happiness, and this is, sad as I sometimes am, suffering as I always am, to find a man superior enough not to ask questions about my life, and to be the lover of my impressions rather than of my body. Such a man I found in the duke; but the duke is old, and old age neither protects nor consoles. I thought I could accept the life which he offered me; but what would you have? I was dying of boredom, and if one is bound to be consumed, it is as well to throw oneself into the flames as to be asphyxiated with charcoal.

'Then I met you, young, ardent, happy, and I tried to make you the man I had longed for in my noisy solitude. What I loved in you was not the man who was, but the man who was going to be. You do not accept the position, you reject it as unworthy of you; you are an ordinary lover. Do like the others; pay me, and say no more about it.'

Marguerite, tired out with this long confession, threw herself back on the sofa, and to stifle a slight cough put up her handkerchief to her lips, and from that to her eyes.

'Pardon, pardon,' I murmured. 'I understood it all, but I wanted to have it from your own lips, my beloved Marguerite. Forget the rest and remember only one thing: that we belong to one another, that we are young, and that we love. Marguerite, do with me as you will; I am your slave, your dog, but in the name of heaven tear up the letter which I wrote to you and do not make me leave you tomorrow; it would kill me.'

Marguerite drew the letter from her bosom, and handing it to me with a smile of infinite sweetness, said:

'Here it is. I have brought it back.'

I tore the letter into fragments and kissed with tears the hand that gave it to me.

At this moment Prudence reappeared.

'Look here, Prudence; do you know what he wants?' said Marguerite.

'He wants you to forgive him.'

'Precisely.'

'And do you?'

'One has to; but he wants more than that.'

'What, then?'

'He wants to have supper with us.'

'And do you consent?'

'What do you think?'

'I think that you are two children who haven't an atom of sense between you; but I also think that I am very hungry, and that the sooner you consent the sooner we shall have supper.'

'Come,' said Marguerite, 'there is room for the three of us in my carriage.'

'By the way,' she added, turning to me, 'Nanine will be gone to bed. You must open the door; take my key, and try not to lose it again.'

I embraced Marguerite until she was almost stifled.

Thereupon Joseph entered.

'Sir,' he said, with the air of a man who is very well satisfied with himself, 'the luggage is packed.'

'All of it?'

'Yes, sir.'

'Well, then, unpack it again; I am not going.'

CHAPTER XVI

I might have told you of the beginning of this *liaison* in a few words, but I wanted you to see every step by which we came, I to agree to whatever Marguerite wished, Marguerite to be unable to live apart from me.

It was the day after the evening when she came to see me that I sent her Manon Lescaut.

From that time, seeing that I could not change my mistress's life, I changed my own. I wished above all not to leave myself time to think over the position I had accepted, for, in spite of myself, it was a great distress to me. Thus my life, generally so calm, assumed all at once an appearance of noise and disorder. Never believe, however disinterested the love of a kept woman may be, that it will cost one nothing. Nothing is so expensive as their caprices, flowers, boxes at the theatre, suppers, days in the country, which one can never refuse to one's mistress.

As I have told you, I had little money. My father was, and still is, treasurer of C. He has a great reputation there for loyalty, thanks to which he was able to find the security and put aside a dowry for my sister. My father is the most honourable man in the world. When my mother died, she left six thousand francs a year, which he divided between my sister and myself on the very day when he received his appointment; then, when I was twenty-one, he added to this little income an annual allowance of five thousand francs, assuring me that with eight thousand francs a year I might live very happily at Paris, if, in addition to this, I would make a postion for myself either in law or medicine. I came to Paris, studied law, was called to the bar, and, like many other young men, put my diploma in my pocket, and let myself drift, as one so easily does in Paris.

My expenses were very moderate; only I used up my year's income in eight months, and spent the four summer months with my father, which practically gave me twelve thousand francs a year, and, in addition, the reputation of a good son. For the rest, not a penny of debt.

This, then, was my position when I made the acquaintance of Marguerite. You can well understand that, in spite of myself, my expenses soon increased. Marguerite's nature was very capricious, and, like so many women, she never regarded as a serious expense those thousand and one distractions which made up her life. So, wishing to spend as much time with me as possible, she would write to me in the morning that she would dine with me, not at home, but at some restaurant in Paris or in the country. I would call for her, and we would dine and go on to the theatre, often having supper as well; and by the end of the evening I had spent four or five louis, which came to two or three thousand francs a month, which reduced my year to three months and a half, and made it necessary for me either to go into debt or to leave Marguerite. I would have consented to anything except the latter.

Forgive me if I give you all these details, but you will see that they were the cause of what was to follow. What I tell you is a true and simple story, and I leave in all the *naïveté* of its details and all the simplicity of its developments.

I realized then that as nothing in the world would make me forget my mistress, it was needful for me to find some way of meeting the expenses into which she drew me. Then, too, my love for her had so disturbing an influence upon me that every moment I spent away from Marguerite was like a year, and that I felt the need of consuming these moments in the fire of some sort of passion, and of living them so swiftly as not to know that I was living them.

I began by borrowing five or six thousand francs on my little capital, and with this I took to gambling. Since gambling houses were destroyed gambling goes on everywhere. Formerly, when one went to Frascati, one had the chance of making a fortune; one played against money, and if one lost, there was always the consolation of saying that one might have gained; whereas now, except in the clubs, where there is still a certain rigour in regard to payments, one is almost certain, the moment one gains a considerable sum, not to receive it. You will readily understand why.

Gambling is only likely to be carried on by young people very much in need of money and not possessing the fortune necessary for supporting the life they lead; they gamble, then, and with this result; a few of them gain, but those who lose serve to pay for their horses and mistresses, which is very disagreeable. Debts are contracted, acquaintances begun about a green table end by quarrels in which life or honour comes to grief; and though one may be an honest man, one finds oneself ruined by other honest men, whose only defect is that they have not two hundred thousand francs a year.

I need not tell you of those who cheat at play, and of how one hears one fine day of their hasty disappearance and tardy condemnation.

I flung myself into this rapid, noisy, and volcanic life, which had formerly terrified me when I thought of it, and which had become for me the necessary complement of my love for Marguerite. What else could I have done?

The nights that I did not spend in the Rue d'Antin, if I had spent them alone in my own room, I could not have slept. Jealousy would have kept me awake, and inflamed my blood and my thoughts; while gambling gave a new turn to the fever which would otherwise have preyed upon my heart, and fixed it upon a passion which laid hold on me in spite of myself, until the hour struck when I might go to my mistress. Then, and by this I knew the violence of my love, I left the table without a moment's hesitation, whether I was winning or losing, pitying those whom I left behind because they would not, like me, find their real happiness in leaving it. For the most of them, gambling was a necessity; for me, it was a remedy. Free of Marguerite, I should have been free of gambling.

Thus, in the midst of that, I preserved a considerable amount of self-possession; I lost only what I was able to pay, and gained only what I should have been able to lose.

For the rest, chance was on my side. I made no debts, and I spent three times as much money as when I did not gamble. It was impossible to resist an existence which gave me an easy means of satisfying the thousand caprices of Marguerite. As for her, she continued to love me as much, or even more than ever.

As I told you, I began by being allowed to stay only from midnight to six o'clock, then I was asked sometimes to a box in the theatre, then she sometimes came to dine with me. One morning I did not go till eight, and there came a day when I did not go till twelve.

But, sooner than the moral metamorphosis, a physical metamorphosis came about in Marguerite. I had taken her cure in hand, and the poor girl, seeing my aim, obeyed me in order to prove her gratitude. I had succeeded without effort or trouble in almost isolating her from her former habits. My doctor, whom I had made her meet, had told me that only rest and calm could preserve her health, so that in place of supper and sleepless nights, I succeeded in substituting a hygienic programme and regular sleep. In spite of herself, Marguerite got accustomed to this new existence, whose salutary effects she had already realized. She began to spend some of her evenings at home, or, if the weather was fine, she wrapped herself in a shawl, put on a veil, and we went on foot, like two children, in the dim alleys of the Champs-Élysées. She would come in tired, take a light supper, and go to bed after a little music or reading, which she had never been used to. The cough, which every time that I heard it seemed to go through my chest, had almost completely disappeared.

At the end of six weeks the count was entirely given up, and only the duke obliged me to conceal my *liaison* with Marguerite, and even he was sent away when I was there, under the pretext that she was asleep and had given orders that she was not to be awakened.

The habit or the need of seeing me which Marguerite had now contracted had this good result: that it forced me to leave the gaming-table just at the moment when an adroit gambler would have left it. Settling one thing against another, I found myself in possession of some ten thousand francs, which seemed to me an inexhaustible capital.

The time of the year when I was accustomed to join my father and sister had now arrived, and I did not go; both of them wrote to me frequently, begging me to come. To these letters I replied as best I could, always repeating that I was quite well and that I was not in need of money, two things which, I thought, would console my father for my delay in paying him my annual visit.

Just then, one fine day in summer, Marguerite was awakened by the sunlight pouring into her room, and jumping out of bed, asked me if I would take her into the country for the whole day.

We sent for Prudence, and all three set off, after Marguerite had given Nanine orders to tell the duke that she had taken advantage of the fine day to go into the country with Mme. Duvernoy.

Besides the presence of Mme. Duvernoy being needful on account of the old duke, Prudence was one of those women who seem made on purpose for days in the country. With her unchanging good-humour and her eternal appetite, she never left a dull moment to those whom she was with, and was perfectly happy in ordering eggs, cherries, milk, stewed rabbit, and all the rest of the traditional lunch in the country.

We had now only to decide where we should go. It was once more Prudence who settled the difficulty.

'Do you want to go to the real country?'

'Yes.'

'Well, let us go to Bougival, at the Point du Jour, at Widow Arnoulds's. Armand, order an open carriage.'

An hour and a half later, we were at Widow Arnould's.

Perhaps you know the inn, which is a hotel on week days and a tea garden on Sundays. There is a magnificent view from the garden, which is at the height of an ordinary first floor. On the left the Aqueduct of Marly closes in the horizon, on the right one looks across hill after hill; the river, almost without current at that spot, unrolls itself like a large white watered ribbon between the plain of the Gabillons and the islands of Croissy, lulled eternally by the trembling of its high poplars and the murmur of its willows. Beyond, distinct in the sunlight, rise little white houses, with red roofs, and factories, which, at that distance, put an admirable finish to the landscape. Beyond that, Paris in the mist! As Prudence had told us, it was the real country, and, I must add, it was a real lunch.

It was not only out of gratitude for the happiness I owe it, but Bougival, in spite of its horrible name, is one of the prettiest places that it is possible to imagine. I have travelled a good deal, and seen much grander things, but none more charming than this little village gaily seated at the foot of the hill which protects it.

Mme. Arnould asked us if we would take a boat, and Marguerite and Prudence accepted joyously.

People have always associated the country with love, and they have done well; nothing affords so fine a frame for the woman whom one loves as the blue sky, the odours, the flowers, the breeze, the shining solitude of fields, or woods. However much one loves a woman, whatever confidence one may have in her, whatever certainty her past may offer us as to her future, one is always more or less jealous. If you have been in love, you must have felt the need of isolating from this world the being in whom you would live wholly. It seems as if, however indifferent she may be to her surroundings, the woman whom one loves loses something of her perfume and of her unity at the contact of men and things. As for me, I experienced that more than most. Mine was not an ordinary love; I was as much in love as an ordinary creature could be, but with Marguerite Gautier; that is to say, that in Paris, at every step, I might elbow the man who had already been her lover or who was about to be. In the country, surrounded by people whom we had never seen and who had no concern with us, alone with Nature in the spring-time of the year, that annual pardon, and shut off from the noise of the city, I could hide my jealousy, and love without shame or fear.

The courtesan disappeared little by little. I had by me a young and beautiful woman, whom I loved, and who loved me, and who was called Marguerite; the past had no more reality and the future no more clouds. The sun shone upon my mistress as it might have shone upon the purest bride. We walked together in those charming spots which seemed to have been made on purpose to recall the verses of Lamartine or to sing the melodies of Scudo. Marguerite was dressed in white, she leaned on my arm, saying over to me again under the starry sky the words she had said to me the day before, and far off the world went on its way, without darkening with its shadow the radiant picture of our youth and love.

That was the dream that the hot sun brought to me that day through the leaves of the trees, as, lying on the grass of the island on which we had landed, I let my thought wander, free from the human links that bound it, gathering to itself every hope that came in its way.

Add to this that, from the place where I was, I could see on the shore a charming little house of two stories, with a semi-circular railing; through the railing, in front of the house, a green lawn, smooth as velvet, and behind the house a little wood full of mysterious retreats, where the moss must efface each morning the pathway that had been made the day before. Climbing flowers clung about the doorway of this uninhabited house, mounting as high as the first storey.

I looked at the house so long that I began by thinking of it as mine, so perfectly did it embody the dream that I was dreaming; I saw Marguerite and myself there, by day in the little wood that covered the hillside, in the evening seated on the grass, and I asked myself if earthly creatures had ever been so happy as we should be.

'What a pretty house!' Marguerite said to me, as she followed the direction of my gaze and perhaps of my thought.

'Where?' asked Prudence.

'Yonder,' and Marguerite pointed to the house in question.

'Ah, delicious!' replied Prudence. 'Do you like it?'

'Very much.'

'Well, tell the duke to take it for you; he would do so, I am sure. I'll see about it if you like.'

Marguerite looked at me, as if to ask me what I thought. My dream vanished at the last words of Prudence, and brought me back to reality so brutally that I was still stunned with the fall.

'Yes, yes, an excellent idea,' I stammered, not knowing what I was saying.

'Well, I will arrange that,' said Marguerite, freeing my hand, and interpreting my words according to her own desire. 'Let us go and see if it is to let.'

The house was empty, and to let for two thousand francs.

'Would you be happy here?' she said to me.

'Am I sure of coming here?'

'And for whom else would I bury myself here, if not for you?'

'Well, then, Marguerite, let me take it myself.'

'You are mad; not only is it unnecessary, but it would be dangerous. You know perfectly well that I have no right to accept it save from one man. Let me alone, big baby, and say nothing.'

'That means,' said Prudence, 'that when I have two days free I will come and spend them with you.'

We left the house, and started on our return to Paris, talking over the new plan. I held Marguerite in my arms, and as I got down from the carriage, I had already begun to look upon her arrangement with less critical eyes.

CHAPTER XVII

Next day Marguerite sent me away very early, saying that the duke was coming at an early hour, and promising to write to me the moment he went, and to make an appointment for the evening. In the course of the day I received this note:

'I am going to Bougival with the duke; be at Prudence's tonight at eight.'

At the appointed hour Marguerite came to me at Mme. Duvernoy's.

'Well, it is all settled,' she said, as she entered.

'The house is taken?' asked Prudence.

'Yes; he agreed at once.'

I did not know the duke, but I felt ashamed of deceiving him.

'But that is not all,' continued Marguerite.

'What else is there?'

'I have been seeing about a place for Armand to stay.'

'In the same house?' asked Prudence, laughing.

'No, at Point du Jour, where we had dinner, the duke and I. While he was admiring the view, I asked Mme. Arnould (she is called Mme. Arnould, isn't she?) if there were any suitable rooms, and she showed me just the very thing: *salon*, anteroom, and bed-room, at sixty francs a month; the whole place furnished in a way to divert a hypochondriac. I took it. Was I right?'

I flung my arms around her neck and kissed her.

'It will be charming,' she continued. 'You have the key of the little door, and I have promised the duke the key of the front door, which he will not take, because he will come during the day when he comes. I think, between ourselves, that he is enchanted with a caprice which will keep me out of Paris for a time, and so silence the objections of his family.

However, he has asked me how I, loving Paris as I do, could make up my mind to bury myself in the country. I told him that I was ill, and that I wanted rest. He seemed to have some difficulty believing me. The poor old man is always on the watch. We must take every precaution, my dear Armand, for he will have me watched while I am there; and it isn't only the question of his taking a house for me, but he has my debts to pay, and unluckily I have plenty. Does all that suit you?'

'Yes,' I answered, trying to quiet the scruples which this way of living awoke in me from time to time.

'We went all over the house, and we shall have everything perfect. The duke is going to look after every single thing. Ah, my dear,' she added, kissing me, 'you're in luck; it's a millionaire who makes your bed for you.'

'And when will you move into the house?' inquired Prudence.

'As soon as possible.'

'Will you take your horses and carriage?'

'I shall take the whole house, and you can look after my place while I am away.'

A week later Marguerite was settled in her country house, and I was installed at the Point du Jour.

Then began an existence which I shall have some difficulty in describing to you. At first Marguerite could not break entirely with her former habits, and, as the house was always festive, all the women whom she knew came to see her. For a whole month there was not a day when Marguerite had not eight or ten people to meals. Prudence, on her side, brought down all the people she knew, and did the honours of the house as if the house belonged to her.

The duke's money paid for all that, as you may imagine; but from time to time Prudence came to me, asking for a note for a thousand francs, professedly on behalf of Marguerite. You know I had won some money at gambling; I therefore immediately handed over to Prudence what she asked for Marguerite, and fearing lest she should require more than I possessed, I borrowed at Paris a sum equal to that which I had already borrowed and paid back. I was then once more in possession of some ten thousand francs, without reckoning my allowance. However, Marguerite's pleasure in seeing her friends was a little moderated when she saw the expense which that pleasure entailed, and especially the necessity she was sometimes in of asking me for money. The duke, who had taken the house in order that Marguerite might rest there, no longer visited it, fearing to find himself in the midst of a large and merry company, by whom he did not wish to be seen. This came about through his having once arrived to dine privately with Marguerite, and having fallen upon a party of fifteen, who were still at lunch at an hour when he was prepared to sit down to dinner. He had unsuspectingly opened the dining-room door, and had been greeted by a burst of laughter, and had had to retire precipitately before the impertinent mirth of the women who were assembled there.

Marguerite rose from the table, and joined the duke in the next room, where she tried, as far as possible, to induce him to forget the incident, but the old man, wounded in his dignity, bore her a grudge for it, and could not forgive her. He said to her, somewhat cruelly, that he was tired of paying for the follies of a woman who could not even have him treated with respect under his own roof, and he went away in great indignation.

Since that day he had never been heard of.

In vain Marguerite dismissed her guests, changed her way of life; the duke still did not come. I was the gainer in so far that my mistress now belonged to me more completely, and my dream was at length realized. Marguerite could not be without me. Not caring what the result might be, she publicly proclaimed our *liaison*, and I had come to live entirely at her house. The servants addressed me officially as their master.

Prudence had strictly sermonized Marguerite in regard to her new manner of life; she had replied that she loved me, that she could not live without me, and that, happen what might, she would not sacrifice the pleasure of having me constantly with her, adding that those who were not satisfied with this arrangement were free to stay away. So much I had heard one day when Prudence had said to Marguerite that she had something very important to tell her, and I had listened at the door of the room into which they had shut themselves.

Not long after, Prudence returned again. I was at the other end of the garden when she arrived, and she did not see me. I had no doubt, from the way in which Marguerite came to meet her, that another similar conversation was about to take place, and I was anxious to hear what it was about. The two women shut themselves into a boudoir, and I put myself within hearing.

'Well?' said Marguerite.

'Well, I have seen the duke.'

'What did he say?'

'That he would gladly forgive you in regard to the scene which took place, but that he had learned that you are publicly living with M. Armand Duval, and that he will never forgive that. "Let Marguerite leave the young man," he said to me, "and, as in the past, I will give her all that she requires; if not, let her ask nothing more from me."'

'And you replied?'

'That I would report his decision to you, and I promised him that I would bring you into a more reasonable frame of mind. Only think, my dear child, of the position that you are losing, and that Armand can never give you. He loves you with all his soul, but he has no fortune capable of supplying your needs, and he will be bound to leave you one day, when it will be too late and when the duke will refuse to do any more for you. Would you like me to speak to Armand?'

Marguerite seemed to be thinking, for she answered nothing. My heart beat violently while I waited for her reply.

'No,' she answered, 'I will not leave Armand, and I will not conceal the fact that I am living with him. It is folly no doubt, but I love him. What would you have me do? And then, now that he has got accustomed to be always with me, he would suffer too cruelly if he had to leave me so much as an hour a day. Besides, I have not such a long time to live that I need make myself miserable in order to please an old man whose very sight makes me feel old. Let him keep his money; I will do without it.'

'But what will you do?'

'I don't in the least know.'

Prudence was no doubt going to make some reply, but I entered suddenly and flung myself at Marguerite's feet, covering her hands with tears in my joy of being thus loved.

'My life is yours, Marguerite; you need this man no longer. Am I not here? Shall I ever leave you, and can I ever repay you for the happiness that you give me? No more barriers, my Marguerite; we love; what matters all the rest?'

'Oh, yes, I love you, Armand,' she murmured, putting her two arms around my neck. 'I love you as I never thought I should ever love. We will be happy; we will live quietly, and I will say good-bye forever to the life for which I now blush. You won't ever reproach me for the past? Tell me!'

Tears choked my voice. I could only reply by clasping Marguerite to my heart.

'Well,' said she, turning to Prudence, and speaking in a broken voice, 'you can report this scene to the duke, and you can add that we have no longer any need of him.'

From that day forth the duke was never referred to. Marguerite was no longer the same woman that I had known. She avoided everything that might recall to me the life which she had been leading when I first met her. Never did wife or sister surround husband or brother with such loving care as she had for me. Her nature was morbidly open to all impressions and accessible to all sentiments. She had broken equally with her friends and with her ways, with her words and with her extravagances. Any one who had seen us leaving the house to go to the river in the charming little boat which I had bought would never have believed that the woman dressed in white, wearing a straw hat, and carrying on her arm a little silk pelisse to protect her against the damp of the river, was that Marguerite Gautier who, only four months ago, had been the talk of the town for the luxury and scandal of her existence.

Alas, we made haste to be happy, as if we knew that we were not to be happy long.

For two months we had not even been to Paris. No one came to see use, except Prudence and Julie Duprat, of whom I have spoken to you, and to whom Marguerite was afterward to give the touching narrative that I have here.

I passed whole days at the feet of my mistress. We opened the windows upon the garden, and as we watched the summer ripening in its flowers and under the shadow of the trees, we breathed together that true life which neither Marguerite nor I have ever known before.

Her delight in the smallest things was like that of a child. There were days when she ran in the garden, like a child of ten, after a butterfly or a dragon-fly. This courtesan who had cost more money in bouquets than would have kept a whole family in comfort, would sometimes sit on the grass for an hour, examining the simple flower whose name she bore.

It was at this time that she read Manon Lescaut, over and over again. I found her several times making notes in the book, and she always declared that when a woman loves, she can not do as Manon did.

The duke wrote to her two or three times. She recognized the writing and gave me the letters without reading them. Sometimes the terms of these letters brought tears to my eyes. He had imagined that by closing his purse to Marguerite, he would bring her back to him; but when he had perceived the uselessness of these means, he could hold out no longer; he wrote and asked that he might see her again, as before, no matter on what conditions.

I read these urgent and repeated letters, and tore them in pieces, without telling Marguerite what they contained and without advising her to see the old man again, though I was half inclined to, so much did I pity him, but I was afraid lest, if I so advised her she should think that I wished the duke, not merely to come and see her again, but to take over the expenses of the house; I feared, above all that she might think me capable of shirking the responsibilities of every consequence to which her love for me might lead her.

It thus came about that the duke, receiving no reply, ceased to write, and that Marguerite and I continued to live together without giving a thought to the future.

CHAPTER XVIII

It would be difficult to give you all the details of our new life. It was made up of a series of little childish events, charming for us but insignificant to any one else. You know what it is to be in love with a woman, you know how it cuts short the days, and with what loving listlessness one drifts into the morrow. You know that forgetfulness of everything which comes of a violent, confident, reciprocated love. Every being who is not the beloved one seems a useless being in creation. One regrets having cast scraps of one's heart to other women, and one can not believe in the possibility of ever pressing another hand than that which one holds between one's hands. The mind admits neither work nor remembrance; nothing, in short, which can distract it from the one thought in which it is ceaselessly absorbed. Every day one discovers in one's mistress a new charm and unknown delights. Existence itself is but the unceasing accomplishment of an unchanging desire; the soul is but the vestal charged to feed the sacred fire of love.

We often went at night-time to sit in the little wood above the house; there we listened to the cheerful harmonies of evening, both of us thinking of the coming hours which should leave us to one another till the dawn of day. At other times we did not get up all day; we did not even let the sunlight enter our room.

The curtains were hermetically closed, and for a moment the external world did not exist for us. Nanine alone had the right to open our door, but only to bring in our meals and even these we took without getting up, interrupting them with laughter and gaiety. To that succeeded a brief sleep, for, disappearing into the depths of our love, we were like two divers who only come to the surface to take breath.

Nevertheless, I surprised moments of sadness, even tears, in Marguerite; I asked her the cause of her trouble, and she answered:

'Our love is not like other loves, my Armand. You love me as if I had never belonged to another, and I tremble lest later on, repenting of your love, and accusing me of my past, you should let me fall back into that life from which you have taken me. I think that now that I have tasted of another life, I should die if I went back to the old one. Tell me that you will never leave me!'

'I swear it!'

At these words she looked at me as if to read in my eyes whether my oath was sincere; then flung herself into my arms, and, hiding her head in my bosom, said to me: 'You don't know how much I love you!'

One evening, seated on the balcony outside the window, we looked at the moon which seemed to rise with difficulty out of its bed of clouds, and we listened to the wind violently rustling the trees; we held each other's hands, and for a whole quarter of an hour we had not spoken, when Marguerite said to me:

'Winter is at hand. Would you like for us to go abroad?'

'Where?'

'To Italy.'

'You are tired of here?'

'I am afraid of the winter; I am particularly afraid of your return to Paris.'

'Why?'

'For many reasons.'

And she went on abruptly, without giving me her reasons for fears:

'Will you go abroad? I will sell all that I have; we will go and live there, and there will be nothing left of what I was; no one will know who I am. Will you?'

'By all means, if you like, Marguerite, let us travel,' I said. 'But where is the necessity of selling things which you will be glad of when we return? I have not a large enough fortune to accept such a sacrifice; but I have enough for us to be able to travel splendidly for five or six months, if that will amuse you the least in the world.'

'After all, no,' she said, leaving the window and going to sit down on the sofa at the other end of the room. 'Why should we spend money abroad? I cost you enough already, here.'

'You reproach me, Marguerite; it isn't generous.'

'Forgive me, my friend,' she said, giving me her hand. 'This thunder weather gets on my nerves; I do not say what I intend to say.'

And after embracing me she fell into a long reverie.

Scenes of this kind often took place, and though I could not discover their cause, I could not fail to see in Marguerite signs of disquietude in regard to the future. She could not doubt my love, which increased day by day, and yet I often found her sad, without being able to get any explanation of the reason, except some physical cause.

Fearing that so monotonous a life was beginning to weary her, I proposed returning to Paris; but she always refused, assuring me that she could not be so happy anywhere as in the country.

Prudence now came but rarely; but she often wrote letters which I never asked to see, though, every time that they came, they seemed to preoccupy Marguerite deeply. I did not know what to think.

One day Marguerite was in her room. I entered. She was writing.

'To whom are you writing?' I asked.

'To Prudence. Do you want to see what I am writing?'

I had a horror of anything that might look like suspicion, and I answered that I had no desire to know what she was writing; and yet I was certain that letter would have explained to me the cause of her sadness.

Next day the weather was splendid. Marguerite proposed to me to take the boat and go as far as the island of Croissy. She seemed very cheerful; when we got back it was five o'clock.

'Mme. Duvernoy has been here,' said Nanine, as she saw us enter.

'She has gone again?'

'Yes, madame, in the carriage; she said it was arranged.'

'Quite right,' said Marguerite sharply. 'Serve the dinner.'

Two days afterward there came a letter from Prudence, and for a fortnight Marguerite seemed to have got rid of her mysterious gloom, for which she constantly asked my forgiveness, now that it no longer existed.

Still the carriage did not return.

'How is it that Prudence does not send you back your carriage?' I asked one day.

'One of the horses is ill, and there are some repairs to be done. It is better to have that done while we are still here, and don't need a carriage, than to wait till we get back to Paris.'

Prudence came two days afterward, and confirmed what Marguerite had said. The two women went for a walk in the garden, and when I joined them they changed the conversation. That night, as she was going, Prudence complained of the cold and asked Marguerite to lend her a shawl.

So a month passed, and all the time Marguerite was more joyous and more affectionate than she had ever been. Nevertheless the carriage did not return, the shawl had not been sent back, and I began to be anxious in spite of myself, and as I knew in which drawer Marguerite put Prudence's letters, I took advantage of a moment when she was at the other end of the garden, went to the drawer, and tried to open it; in vain, for it was locked. When I opened the drawer in which the trinkets and diamonds were usually kept, these opened without resistance, but the jewel cases had disappeared, along with their contents no doubt.

A sharp fear penetrated my heart. I might indeed ask Marguerite for the truth in regard to these disappearances, but it was certain that she would not confess it.

'My good Marguerite,' I said to her, 'I am going to ask your permission to go to Paris. They do not know my address, and I expect there are letters from my father waiting for me. I have no doubt he is concerned; I ought to answer him.'

'Go, my friend,' she said; 'but be back early.'

I went straight to Prudence.

'Come,' said I, without beating about the bush, 'tell me frankly, where are Marguerite's horses?'

'Sold.'

'The shawl?'

'Sold.'

'The diamonds?'

'Pawned.'

'And who has sold and pawned them?'

'I.'

'Why did you not tell me?'

'Because Marguerite made me promise not to.'

'And why did you not ask me for money?'

'Because she wouldn't let me.'

'And where has the money gone?'

'In payments.'

'Is she much in debt?'

'Thirty thousand francs, or thereabouts. Ah, my dear fellow, didn't I tell you? You wouldn't believe me; now you are convinced. The upholsterer whom the duke had agreed to settle with was shown out of the house when he presented himself, and the duke wrote next day to say that he would answer for nothing in regard to Mlle. Gautier. This man wanted his money; he was given part payment out of the few thousand francs that I got from you; then some kind souls warned him that his debtor had been abandoned by the duke and was living with a penniless young man; the other creditors were told the same; they asked for their money, and seized some of the goods. Marguerite wanted to sell everything, but it was too late, and besides I should have opposed it. But it was necessary to pay, and in order not to ask you for money, she sold her horses and her shawls, and pawned her jewels. Would you like to see the receipts and the pawn tickets?'

And Prudence opened the drawer and showed me the papers.

'Ah, you think,' she continued, with the insistence of a woman who can say, I was right after all. 'Ah, you think it is enough to be in love, and go into the country and lead a dreamy, pastoral life. No, my friend, no. By the side of that ideal life, there is a material life, and the purest resolutions are held to earth by threads which seem slight enough, but which are of iron, not easily to be broken. If Marguerite has not been unfaithful to you twenty times, it is because she has an exceptional nature. It is not my fault for not advising her to, for I couldn't bear to see the poor girl stripping herself of everything. She wouldn't; she replied that she loved you, and she wouldn't be unfaithful to you for anything in the world. All that is very pretty, very poetical, but one can't pay one's creditors in that coin, and now she can't free herself from debt, unless she can raise thirty thousand francs.'

'All right, I will provide that amount.'

'You will borrow it?'

'Good heavens! Why, yes!'

'A fine thing that would be to do; you will fall out with your father, cripple your resources, and one doesn't find thirty thousand francs from one day to another. Believe me, my dear Armand, I know women better than you do; do not commit this folly; you will be sorry for it one day. Be reasonable. I don't advise you to leave Marguerite, but live with her as you did at the beginning. Let her find the means to get out of this difficulty. The duke will come back in a little while. The Comte de N., if she would take him, he told me yesterday even, would pay all her debts, and give her four or five thousand francs a month. He has two hundred thousand francs a year. It would be a position for her, while you will certainly be obliged to leave her. Don't wait till you are ruined, especially as the Comte. de N. is a fool, and nothing would prevent your still being Marguerite's lover. She would cry a little at the beginning, but she would come to accustom herself to it, and you would thank me one day for what you had done. Imagine that Marguerite is married, and deceive the husband; that is all. I have already told you all this once, only at that time it was merely advice, and now it is almost a necessity.'

What Prudence said was cruelly true.

'This is how it is,' she went on, putting away the papers she had just shown me; 'women like Marguerite always foresee that some one will love them, never that they will love; otherwise they would put aside money, and at thirty they could afford the luxury of a lover for nothing. If I had only known once what I know now! In short, say nothing to Marguerite, and bring her back to Paris. You have lived with her alone for four or five months; that is quite enough. Shut your eyes now; that is all that any one asks of you. At the end of a fortnight she will take the Comte de N., and she will save up during the winter, and next summer you will begin over again. That is how things are done, my dear fellow!'

And Prudence appeared to be enchanted with her advice, which I refused indignantly.

Not only my love and my dignity would not let me act thus, but I was certain that, feeling as she did now, Marguerite would die rather than accept another lover.

'Enough joking,' I said to Prudence; 'tell me exactly how much Marguerite is in need of.'

'I have told you: thirty thousand francs.'

'And when does she require this sum?'

'Before the end of two months.'

'She shall have it.'

Prudence shrugged her shoulders.

'I will give it to you,' I continued, 'but you must swear to me that you will not tell Marguerite that I have given it to you.'

'Don't be afraid.'

'And if she sends you anything else to sell or pawn, let me know.'

'There is no danger. She has nothing left.'

I went straight to my own house to see if there were any letters from my father. There were four.

CHAPTER XIX

In his first three letters my father inquired the cause of my silence; in the last he allowed me to see that he had heard of my change of life, and informed me that he was about to come and see me.

I have always had a great respect and a sincere affection for my father. I replied that I had been travelling for a short time, and begged him to let me know beforehand what day he would arrive, so that I could be there to meet him.

I gave my servant my address in the country, telling him to bring me the first letter that came with the post-mark of C., then I returned to Bougival.

Marguerite was waiting for me at the garden gate. She looked at me anxiously. Throwing her arms around my neck, she said to me: 'Have you seen Prudence?'

'No.'

'You were a long time in Paris.'

'I found letters from my father to which I had to reply.'

A few minutes afterward Nanine entered, all out of breath, Marguerite rose and talked with her in whispers. When Nanine had gone out Marguerite sat down by me again and said, taking my hand:

'Why did you deceive me? You went to see Prudence.'

'Who told you?'

'Nanine.'

'And how did she know?'

'She followed you.'

'You told her to follow me?'

'Yes. I thought that you must have had a very strong motive for going to Paris, after not leaving me for four months. I was afraid that something might happen to you or that you were perhaps going to see another woman.'

'Child!'

'Now I am relieved. I know what you have done, but I don't yet know what you have been told.'

I showed Marguerite my father's letters.

'This is not what I am asking you about. What I want to know is why you went to see Prudence.'

'To see her.'

'That's a lie, my friend.'

'Well, I went to ask her if the horse was any better, and if she wanted your shawl and your jewels any longer.'

Marguerite blushed, but did not answer.

'And,' I continued, 'I learned what you had done with your horses, shawls, and jewels.'

'And you are vexed?'

'I am vexed that it never occurred to you to ask me for what you were in want of.'

'In a *liaison* like ours, if the woman has any sense of dignity at all, she ought to make every possible sacrifice rather than ask her lover for money and so give a venal character to her love. You love me, I am sure, but you do not know on how slight a thread depends the love one has for a woman like me. Who knows? Perhaps some day when you were bored or worried you would fancy you saw a carefully concerted plan in our *liaison*. Prudence is a chatterbox. What need had I of the horses? It was an economy to sell them. I don't use them and I don't spend anything on their keep; if you love me, I ask nothing more, and you will love me just as much without horses, or shawls, or diamonds.'

All that was said so naturally that the tears came to my eyes as I listened.

'But, my good Marguerite,' I replied, pressing her hands lovingly, 'you knew that one day I should discover the sacrifice you had made, and that the moment I discovered it I should allow it no longer.'

'But why?'

'Because, my dear child, I can not allow your affection for me to deprive you of even a trinket. I too should not like you to be able, in a moment when you were bored or worried, to think that if you were living with somebody else those moments would not exist; and to repent, if only for a minute, of living with me. In a few days your horses, your diamonds, and your shawls shall be returned to you. They are as necessary to you as air is to life, and it may be absurd, but I like you better showy than simple.'

'Then you no longer love me.'

'Foolish creature!'

'If you loved me, you would let me love you my own way; on the contrary, you persist in only seeing in me a woman to whom luxury is indispensable, and whom you think you are always obliged to pay. You are ashamed to accept the proof of my love. In spite of yourself, you think of leaving me some day, and you want to put your disinterestedness beyond risk of suspicion. You are right, my friend, but I had better hopes.'

And Marguerite made a motion to rise; I held her, and said to her:

'I want you to be happy and to have nothing to reproach me for, that is all.'

'And we are going to be separated!'

'Why Marguerite, who can separate us?' I cried.

'You, who will not let me take you on your own level, but insist on taking me on mine; you, who wish me to keep the luxury in the midst of which I have lived, and so keep the moral distance which separates us; you, who do not believe that my affection is sufficiently disinterested to share with me what you have, though we could live happily enough on it together, and would rather ruin yourself, because you are still bound by a foolish prejudice. Do you really think that I could compare a carriage and diamonds with your love? Do you think that my real happiness lies in the trifles that mean so much when one has nothing to love, but which become trifling indeed when one has? You will pay my debts, realize your estate, and then keep me? How long will that last? Two or three months, and then it will be too late to live the life I propose, for then you will have to take everything from me, and that is what a man of honour can not do; while now you have eight or ten thousand francs a year, on which we should be able to live. I will sell the rest of what I do not want, and with this alone I will make two thousand francs a year. We will take a nice little flat in which we can both live. In the summer we will go into the country, not to a house like this, but to a house just big enough for two people. You are independent, I am free, we are young; in heaven's name, Armand, do not drive me back into the life I had to lead once!'

I could not answer. Tears of gratitude and love filled my eyes, and I flung myself into Marguerite's arms.

'I wanted,' she continued, 'to arrange everything without telling you, pay all my debts, and take a new flat. In October we should have been back in Paris, and all would have come out; but since Prudence has told you all, you will have to agree beforehand, instead of agreeing afterward. Do you love me enough for that?'

It was impossible to resist such devotion. I kissed her hands ardently, and said:

'I will do whatever you wish.'

It was agreed that we should do as she had planned. Thereupon, she went wild with delight; danced, sang, amused herself with calling up pictures of her new flat in all its simplicity, and began to consult me as to its position and arrangement. I saw how happy and proud she was of this resolution, which seemed as if it would bring us into closer and closer relationship, and I resolved to do my own share. In an instant I decided the whole course of my life. I put my affairs in order, and made over to Marguerite the income which had come to me from my mother, and which seemed little enough in return for the sacrifice which I was accepting. There remained the five thousand francs a year from my father; and, whatever happened, I had always enough to live on. I did not tell Marguerite what I had done, certain as I was that she would refuse the gift. This income came from a mortgage of sixty thousand francs on a house that I had never even seen. All that I knew was that every three months my father's solicitor, an old friend of the family, handed over to me seven hundred and fifty francs in return for my receipt.

The day when Marguerite and I came to Paris to look for a flat, I went to this solicitor and asked him what had to be done in order to make over this income to another person. The good man imagined I was ruined, and questioned me as to the cause of my decision. As I knew that I should be obliged, sooner or later, to say in whose favour I made this transfer, I thought it best to tell him the truth at once. He made none of the objections that his position as friend and solicitor authorized him to make, and assured me that he would arrange the whole affair in the best way possible. Naturally I begged him to employ the greatest discretion in regard to my father, and on leaving him I rejoined Marguerite, who was waiting for me at Julie Duprat's, where she had gone in preference to going to listen to the moralizings of Prudence.

We began to look for flats. All those that we saw seemed to Marguerite too dear, and to me too simple. However, we finally found, in one of the quietest parts of Paris, a little house, isolated from the main part of the building. Behind this little house was a charming garden, surrounded by walls high enough to screen us from our neighbours and low enough not to shut off our own view. It was better than our expectations.

While I went to give notice at my own flat, Marguerite went to see a business agent, who, she told me, had already done for one of her friends exactly what she wanted him to do for her. She came on to the Rue de Provence in a state of great delight. The man had promised to pay all her debts, to give her a receipt for the amount, and to hand over twenty thousand francs, in return for the whole of her furniture. You have seen by the amount taken at the sale that this honest man would have gained thirty thousand francs out of his client.

We went back joyously to Bougival, talking over our projects for the future, which, thanks to our heedlessness, and especially to our love, we saw in the rosiest light.

A week later, as we were having lunch, Nanine came to tell us that my servant was asking for me. 'Let him come in,' I said.

'Sir,' said he, 'your father has arrived in Paris, and begs you to return at once to your rooms, where he is waiting for you.'

This piece of news was the most natural thing in the world, yet, as we heard it, Marguerite and I looked at one another. We foresaw trouble. Before she had spoken a word, I replied to her thought, and, taking her hand, I said, 'Fear nothing.'

'Come back as soon as possible,' whispered Marguerite, embracing me; 'I will wait for you at the window.'

I sent Joseph to tell my father that I was on my way. Two hours later I was at the Rue de Provence.

CHAPTER XX

My father was seated in my room in his dressing-gown; he was writing, and I saw at once, by the way in which he raised his eyes to me when I came in, that there was going to be a serious discussion. I went up to him, all the same, as if I had seen nothing in his face, embraced him, and said:

'When did you come, father?'

'Last night.'

'Did you come straight here, as usual?'

'Yes.'

'I am very sorry not to have been here to receive you.'

I expected that the sermon which my father's cold face threatened would begin at once; but he said nothing, sealed the letter which he had just written, and gave it to Joseph to post.

When we were alone, my father rose, and leaning against the mantelpiece, said to me:

'My dear Armand, we have serious matters to discuss.'

'I am listening, father.'

'You promise me to be frank?'

'Am I not accustomed to be so?'

'Is it not true that you are living with a woman called Marguerite Gautier?'

'Yes.'

'Do you know what this woman was?'

'A kept woman.'

'And it is for her that you have forgotten to come and see your sister and me this year?'

'Yes, father, I admit it.'

'You are very much in love with this woman?'

'You see it, father, since she has made me fail in duty toward you, for which I humbly ask your forgiveness today.'

My father, no doubt, was not expecting such categorical answers, for he seemed to reflect a moment, and then said to me:

'You have, of course, realized that you can not always live like that?'

'I fear so, father, but I have not realized it.'

'But you must realize,' continued my father, in a dryer tone, 'that I, at all events, should not permit it.'

'I have said to myself that as long as I did nothing contrary to the respect which I owe to the traditional probity of the family I could live as I am living, and this has reassured me somewhat in regard to the fears I have had.'

Passions are formidable enemies to sentiment. I was prepared for every struggle, even with my father, in order that I might keep Marguerite.

'Then the moment is come when you must live otherwise.'

'Why, father?'

'Because you are doing things which outrage the respect that you imagine you have for your family.'

'I don't follow your meaning.'

'I will explain it to you. Have a mistress if you will; pay her as a man of honour is bound to pay the woman whom he keeps, by all means; but that you should come to forget the most sacred things for her, that you should let the report of your scandalous life reach my quiet countryside, and set a blot on the honourable name that I have given you, it can not, it shall not be.'

'Permit me to tell you, father, that those who have given you information about me have been ill-informed. I am the lover of Mlle. Gautier; I live with her; it is the most natural thing in the world. I do not give Mlle. Gautier the name you have given me; I spend on her account what my means allow me to spend; I have no debts; and, in short, I am not in a position which authorizes a father to say to his son what you have just said to me.'

'A father is always authorized to rescue his son out of evil paths. You have not done any harm yet, but you will do it.'

'Father!'

'Sir, I know more of life than you do. There are no entirely pure sentiments except in perfectly chaste women. Every Manon can have her own Des Grieux, and times are changed. It would be useless for the world to grow older if it did not correct its ways. You will leave your mistress.'

'I am very sorry to disobey you, father, but it is impossible.'

'I will compel you to do so.'

'Unfortunately, father, there no longer exists a Sainte-Marguerite to which courtesans can be sent, and, even if there were, I would follow Mlle. Gautier if you succeeded in having her sent there. What would you have? Perhaps I am in the wrong, but I can only be happy as long as I am the lover of this woman.'

'Come Armand, open your eyes. Recognize that it is your father who speaks to you, your father who has always loved you, and who only desires your happiness. Is it honourable for you to live like husband and wife with a woman whom everybody has had?'

'What does it matter, father, if no one will any more? What does it matter, if this woman loves me, if her whole life is changed through the love which she has for me and the love which I have for her? What does it matter, if she has become a different woman?'

'Do you think, then, sir, that the mission of a man of honour is to go about converting lost women? Do you think that God has given such a grotesque aim to life, and that the heart should have any room for enthusiasm of that kind? What will be the end of this marvellous cure, and what will you think of what you are saying today by the time you are forty? You will laugh at this love of yours, if you can still laugh, and if it has not left too serious a trace in your past. What would you be now if your father had had your ideas and had given up his life to every impulse of this kind, instead of rooting himself firmly in convictions of honour and steadfastness? Think it over, Armand, and do not talk any more such absurdities. Come, leave this woman; your father entreats you.'

I answered nothing.

'Armand,' continued my father, 'in the name of your sainted mother, abandon this life, which you will forget more easily than you think. You are tied to it by an impossible theory. You are twenty-four; think of the future. You can not always love this woman, who also can not always love you. You both exaggerate your love. You put an end to your whole career. One step further, and you will no longer be able to leave the path you have chosen, and you will suffer all your life for what you have done in your youth. Leave Paris. Come and stay for a month or two with your sister and me. Rest in our quiet family affection will soon heal you of this fever, for it is nothing else. Meanwhile, your mistress will console herself; she will take another lover; and when you see what it is for which you have all but broken with your father, and all but lost his love, you will tell me that I have done well to come and seek you out, and you will thank me for it. Come, you will go with me, Armand, will you not?'

I felt that my father would be right if it had been any other woman, but I was convinced that he was wrong with regard to Marguerite. Nevertheless, the tone in which he said these last words was so kind, so appealing, that I dared not answer.

'Well?' said he in a trembling voice.

'Well, father, I can promise nothing,' I said at last; 'what you ask of me is beyond my power. Believe me,' I continued, seeing him make an impatient move, 'you exaggerate the effects of this *liaison*. Marguerite is a different kind of woman from what you think. This love, far from leading me astray, is capable, on the contrary, of setting me in the right direction. Love always makes a man better, no matter what woman inspires it. If you knew Marguerite, you would understand that I am in no danger. She is as noble as the noblest of women. There is as much disinterestedness in her as there is cupidity in others.'

'All of which does not prevent her from accepting the whole of your fortune, for the sixty thousand francs which came to you from your mother, and which you are giving her, are, understand me well, your whole fortune.'

My father had probably kept this peroration and this threat for the last stroke. I was firmer before these threats than before his entreaties.

'Who told you that I was handing this sum to her?' I asked.

'My solicitor. Could an honest man carry out such a procedure without warning me? Well, it is to prevent you from ruining yourself for a prostitute that I am now in Paris. Your mother, when she died, left you enough to live on respectably, and not to squander on your mistresses.'

'I swear to you, father, that Marguerite knew nothing of this transfer.'

'Why, then, do you make it?'

'Because Marguerite, the woman you calumniate, and whom you wish me to abandon, is sacrificing all that she possesses in order to live with me.'

'And you accept this sacrifice? What sort of a man are you, sir, to allow Mlle. Gautier to sacrifice anything for you? Come, enough of this. You will leave this woman. Just now I begged you; now I command you. I will have no scandalous doings in my family. Pack up your things and get ready to come with me.'

'Pardon me, father,' I said, 'but I shall not come.'

'And why?'

'Because I am at an age when no one any longer obeys a command.'

My father turned pale at my answer.

'Very well, sir,' he said, 'I know what remains to be done.'

He rang and Joseph appeared.

'Have my things taken to the Hôtel de Paris,' he said to my servant. And thereupon he went to his room and finished dressing. When he returned, I went up to him.

'Promise me, father,' I said, 'that you will do nothing to give Marguerite pain?'

My father stopped, looked disdainfully, and contented himself with saying, 'I believe you are mad.' After this he went out, shutting the door violently after him.

I went downstairs, took a cab, and returned to Bougival. Marguerite was waiting for me at the window.

CHAPTER XXI

'At last you have come,' she said, throwing her arms around my neck. 'But how pale you are!'

I told her of the scene with my father.

'My God! I was afraid of it,' she said. 'When Joseph came to tell you of your father's arrival I trembled as if he had brought news of some misfortune. My poor friend, I am the cause of all your distress. You will be better off, perhaps, if you leave me and do not quarrel with your father on my account. He knows that you are sure to have a mistress, and he ought to be thankful that it is I, since I love you and do not want more of you than your position allows. Did you tell him how we had arranged our future?'

'Yes; that is what annoyed him the most, for he saw how much we really love one another.'

'What are we to do, then?'

'Hold together, my good Marguerite, and let the storm pass over.'

'Will it pass?'

'It will have to.'

'But your father will not stop there.'

'What do you suppose he can do?'

'How do I know? Everything that a father can do to make his son obey him. He will remind you of my past life, and will perhaps do me the honour of inventing some new story, so that you may give me up.'

'You know that I love you.'

'Yes, but what I know, too, is that, sooner or later, you will have to obey your father, and perhaps you will end by believing him.'

'No, Marguerite. It is I who will make him believe me. Some of his friends have been telling him tales which have made him angry; but he is good and just, he will change his first impression; and then, after all, what does it matter to me?'

'Do not say that, Armand. I would rather anything should happen than that you should quarrel with your family; wait till after today, and tomorrow go back to Paris. Your father, too, will have thought it over on his side, and perhaps you will both come to a better understanding. Do not go against his principles, pretend to make some concessions to what he wants; seem not to care so very much about me, and he will let things remain as they are. Hope, my friend, and be sure of one thing, that whatever happens, Marguerite will always be yours.'

'You swear it?'

'Do I need to swear it?'

How sweet it is to let oneself be persuaded by the voice that one loves! Marguerite and I spent the whole day in talking over our projects for the future, as if we felt the need of realizing them as quickly as possible. At every moment we awaited some event, but the day passed without bringing us any new tidings.

Next day I left at ten o'clock, and reached the hotel about twelve. My father had gone out.

I went to my own rooms, hoping that he had perhaps gone there. No one had called. I went to the solicitor's. No one was there. I went back to the hotel, and waited till six. M. Duval did not return, and I went back to Bougival.

I found Marguerite not waiting for me, as she had been the day before, but sitting by the fire, which the weather still made necessary. She was so absorbed in her thoughts that I came close to her chair without her hearing me. When I put my lips to her forehead she started as if the kiss had suddenly awakened her.

'You frightened me,' she said. 'And your father?'

'I have not seen him. I do not know what it means. He was not at his hotel, nor anywhere where there was a chance of my finding him.'

'Well, you must try again tomorrow.'

'I am very much inclined to wait till he sends for me. I think I have done all that can be expected of me.'

'No, my friend, it is not enough; you must call on your father again, and you must call tomorrow.'

'Why tomorrow rather than any other day?'

'Because,' said Marguerite, and it seemed to me that she blushed slightly at this question, 'because it will show that you are the more keen about it, and he will forgive us the sooner.'

For the remainder of the day Marguerite was sad and preoccupied. I had to repeat twice over everything I said to her to obtain an answer. She ascribed this preoccupation to her anxiety in regard to the events which had happened during the last two days. I spent the night in reassuring her, and she sent me away in the morning with an insistent disquietude that I could not explain to myself.

Again my father was absent, but he had left this letter for me:

'If you call again today, wait for me till four. If I am not in by four, come and dine with me tomorrow. I must see you.'

I waited till the hour he had named, but he did not appear. I returned to Bougival.

The night before I had found Marguerite sad; that night I found her feverish and agitated. On seeing me, she flung her arms around my neck, but she cried for a long time in my arms. I questioned her as to this sudden distress which alarmed me by its violence. She gave me no positive reason, but put me off with those evasions which a woman resorts to when she will not tell the truth.

When she was a little calmed down, I told her the result of my visit, and showed her my father's letter, from which, I said, we might augur well. At the sight of the letter and on hearing my comment, her tears began to flow so copiously that I feared an attack of nerves, and, calling Nanine, I put her to bed, where she wept without a word, but held my hands and kissed them every moment.

I asked Nanine if, during my absence, her mistress had received any letter or visit which could account for the state in which I found her, but Nanine replied that no one had called and nothing had been sent.

Something, however, had occurred since the day before, something which troubled me the more because Marguerite concealed it from me.

In the evening she seemed a little calmer, and, making me sit at the foot of the bed, she told me many times how much she loved me. She smiled at me, but with an effort, for in spite of herself her eyes were veiled with tears.

I used every means to make her confess the real cause of her distress, but she persisted in giving me nothing but vague reasons, as I have told you. At last she fell asleep in my arms, but it was the sleep which tires rather than rests the body. From time to time she uttered a cry, started up, and, after assuring herself that I was beside her, made me swear that I would always love her.

I could make nothing of these intermittent paroxysms of distress, which went on till morning. Then Marguerite fell into a kind of stupor. She had not slept for two nights.

Her rest was of short duration, for toward eleven she awoke, and, seeing that I was up, she looked about her, crying:

'Are you going already?'

'No,' said I, holding her hands; 'but I wanted to let you sleep on. It is still early.'

'What time are you going to Paris?'

'At four.'

'So soon? But you will stay with me till then?'

'Of course. Do I not always?'

'I am so glad! Shall we have lunch?' she went on absent-mindedly.

'If you like.'

'And then you will be nice to me till the very moment you go?'

'Yes; and I will come back as soon as I can.'

'You will come back?' she said, looking at me with haggard eyes.

'Naturally.'

'Oh, yes, you will come back tonight. I shall wait for you, as I always do, and you will love me, and we shall be happy, as we have been ever since we have known each other.'

All these words were said in such a strained voice they seemed to hide so persistent and so sorrowful a thought, that I trembled every moment lest Marguerite should become delirious.

'Listen,' I said. 'You are ill. I can not leave you like this. I will write and tell my father not to expect me.'

'No, no,' she cried hastily, 'don't do that. Your father will accuse me of hindering you again from going to see him when he wants to see you; no, no, you must go, you must! Besides, I am not ill. I am quite well. I had a bad dream and am not yet fully awake.'

From that moment Marguerite tried to seem more cheerful. There were no more tears.

When the hour came for me to go, I embraced her and asked her if she would come with me as far as the train; I hoped that the walk would distract her and that the air would do her good. I wanted especially to be with her as long as possible.

She agreed, put on her cloak and took Nanine with her, so as not to return alone. Twenty times I was on the point of not going. But the hope of a speedy return, and the fear of offending my father still more, sustained me, and I took my place in the train.

'Till this evening!' I said to Marguerite, as I left her.

She did not reply.

Once already she had not replied to the same words, and the Comte de G., you will remember, had spent the night with her; but that time was so far away that it seemed to have been effaced from my memory, and if I had any fear, it was certainly not of Marguerite being unfaithful to me. Reaching Paris, I hastened off to see Prudence, intending to ask her to go and keep Marguerite company, in the hope that her mirth and liveliness would distract her. I entered without being announced, and found Prudence at her toilet.

'Ah!' she said anxiously; 'is Marguerite with you?'

'No.'

'How is she?'

'She is not well.'

'Is she not coming?'

'Did you expect her?'

Madame Duvernoy reddened, and replied, with a certain constraint:

'I only meant that since you are in Paris, is she not coming to join you?'

'No.'

I looked at Prudence; she cast down her eyes, and I read in her face the fear of seeing my visit prolonged.

'I even came to ask you, my dear Prudence, if you have nothing to do this evening, to go and see Marguerite; you will be company for her, and you can stay the night. I never saw her as she was today, and I am afraid she is going to be ill.'

'I am dining in town,' replied Prudence, 'and I can't go and see Marguerite this evening. I will see her tomorrow.'

I took leave of Mme. Duvernoy, who seemed almost as preoccupied as Marguerite, and went on to my father's; his first glance seemed to study me attentively. He held out his hand.

'Your two visits have given me pleasure, Armand,' he said; 'they make me hope that you have thought over things on your side as I have on mine.'

'May I ask you, father, what was the result of your reflection?'

'The result, my dear boy, that I have exaggerated the importance of the reports that had been made to me, and that I have made up my mind to be less severe with you.'

'What are you saying, father?' I cried joyously.

'I say, my dear child that every young man must have his mistress, and that, from the fresh information I have had, I would rather see you the lover of Mlle. Gautier than of any one else.'

'My dear father, how happy you make me!'

We talked in this manner for some moments, and then sat down to table. My father was charming all dinner time.

I was in a hurry to get back to Bougival to tell Marguerite about this fortunate change, and I looked at the clock every moment.

'You are watching the time,' said my father, 'and you are impatient to leave me. O young people, how you always sacrifice sincere to doubtful affections!'

'Do not say that, father; Marguerite loves me, I am sure of it.'

My father did not answer; he seemed to say neither yes nor no.

He was very insistent that I should spend the whole evening with him and not go till the morning; but Marguerite had not been well when I left her. I told him of it, and begged his permisssion to go back to her early, promising to come again tomorrow.

The weather was fine; he walked with me as far as the station. Never had I been so happy. The future appeared as I had long desired to see it. I had never loved my father as I loved him at that moment.

'You are really very much in love with her?' he said.

'Madly.'

'Go, then,' and he passed his hand across his forehead as if to chase a thought, then opened his mouth as if to say something; but he only pressed my hand, and left me hurriedly, saying:

'Till tomorrow then!'

CHAPTER XXII

It seemed to me as if the train did not move. I reached Bougival at eleven.

Not a window in the house was lighted up, and when I rang no one answered the bell. It was the first time that such a thing had occurred to me. At last the gardener came. I entered. Nanine met me with a light. I went to Marguerite's room.

'Where is madame?'

'Gone to Paris,' replied Nanine.

'To Paris!'

'Yes, sir.'

'When?'

'An hour after you.'

'She left no word for me?'

'Nothing.'

Nanine left me.

Perhaps she had some suspicion or other, I thought, and went to Paris to make sure that my visit to my father was not an excuse for a day off. Perhaps Prudence wrote to her about something important, I said to myself when I was alone; but I saw Prudence; she said nothing to make me suppose that she had written to Marguerite.

All at once I remembered Mme. Duvernoy's question, 'Isn't she coming today?' when I had said that Marguerite was ill. I remembered at the same time how embarrassed Prudence had appeared when I looked at her after this remark, which seemed to indicate an appointment. I remembered, too, Marguerite's tears all day long, which my father's kind reception had rather put out of my mind. From this moment all the incidents grouped themselves about my first suspicion, and fixed it so firmly in my mind that everything served to confirm it, even my father's kindness.

Marguerite has almost insisted on my going to Paris; she had pretended to be calmer when I had proposed staying with

144

her. Had I fallen into some trap? Was Marguerite deceiving me? Had she counted on being back in time for me not to perceive her absence, and had she been detained by chance? Why had she said nothing to Nanine, or why had she not written? What was the meaning of those tears, this absence, this mystery?

That is what I asked myself in affright, as I stood in the vacant room, gazing at the clock, which pointed to midnight, and seemed to say to me that it was too late to hope for my mistress's return. Yet, after all the arrangements we had just made, the sacrifices that had been offered and accepted, was it likely that she was deceiving me? No. I tried to get rid of my first supposition.

Probably she had found a purchaser for her furniture, and she had gone to Paris to conclude the bargain. She did not wish to tell me beforehand, for she knew that, though I had consented to it, the sale so necessary for our future happiness, was painful to me, and feared to wound my self-respect in speaking to me about it. She would rather not see me till the whole thing was done, and that was evidently why Prudence was expecting her when she let out the secret. Marguerite could not finish the whole business today, and was staying the night with Prudence, or perhaps she would come even now for she must know how anxious I should be, and would not wish to leave me in that condition. But, if so, why those tears? No doubt, despite her love for me, the poor girl could not make up her mind to give up all the luxury in which she had lived until now, and for which she had been so envied, without crying over it. I was quite ready to forgive her for such regrets. I waited for her impatiently, that I might say to her, as I covered her with kisses, that I had guessed the reason of her mysterious absence.

Nevertheless, the night went on, and Marguerite did not return.

My anxiety tightened its circle little by little, and began to oppress my head and heart. Perhaps something had happened to her. Perhaps she was injured, ill, dead. Perhaps a messenger would arrive with the news of some dreadful accident. Perhaps the daylight would find me with the same uncertainty and the same fears.

The idea that Marguerite was perhaps unfaithful to me at the very moment when I waited for her in terror at her absence did not return to my mind. There must be some cause, independent of her will, to keep her away from me, and the more I thought, the more convinced I was that this cause could only be some mishap or other. O vanity of man, coming back to us in every form!

One o'clock struck. I said to myself that I would wait another hour, but that at two o'clock, if Marguerite had not returned, I would set out for Paris. Meanwhile I looked about for a book, for I dared not think. Manon Lescaut was open on the table. It seemed to me that here and there the pages were wet as if with tears. I turned the leaves over and then closed the book for the letters seemed to me void of meaning through the veil of my doubt.

Time went slowly. The sky was covered with clouds. An autumn rain lashed the windows. The empty bed seemed at moments to assume the aspect of a tomb. I was afraid.

I opened the door. I listened, and heard nothing but the voice of the wind in the trees. Not a vehicle was to be seen on the road. The half hour sounded sadly from the church tower.

I began to fear lest some one should enter. It seemed to me that only a disaster could come at that hour and under that sombre sky.

Two o'clock struck. I still waited a little. Only the sound of the bell troubled the silence with its monotonous and rhythmical stroke.

At last I left the room, where every object had assumed that melancholy aspect which the restless solitude of the heart gives to all its surroundings.

In the next room I found Nanine sleeping over her work. At the sound of the door, she awoke and asked if her mistress had come in.

'No; but if she comes in, tell her that I was so anxious that I had to go to Paris.'

'At this hour?'

'Yes.'

'But how? You won't find a carriage.'

'I will walk.'

'But it is raining.'

'No matter.'

'But madame will be coming back, or if she doesn't come it will be time enough in the morning to go and see what has kept her. You will be murdered on the way.'

'There is no danger my dear Nanine; I will see you tomorrow.'

The good girl went and got me a cloak, put it over my shoulders, and offered to wake up Mme. Arnould to see if a vehicle could be obtained; but I would hear of nothing, convinced as I was that I should lose, in a perhaps fruitless inquiry, more time than I should take to cover half the road. Besides, I felt the need of air and physical fatigue in order to cool down the over excitement which possessed me.

I took the key of the flat in the Rue d'Antin, and after saying good-bye to Nanine, who came with me as far as the gate, I set out.

At first I began to run, but the earth was muddy with rain, and I fatigued myself doubly. At the end of half an hour I was obliged to stop, and I was drenched with sweat. I recovered my breath and went on. The night was so dark that at every step I feared to dash myself against one of the trees on the roadside, which rose up sharply before me like great phantoms rushing upon me.

I overtook one or two wagons, which I soon left behind. A carriage was going at full gallop towards Bougival. As it passed me the hope came to me that Marguerite was in it. I stopped and cried out, 'Marguerite, Marguerite!' But no one answered and the carriage continued its course. I watched it fade away in the distance, and then started on my way again. I took two hours to reach the Barrière de l'Étoile. The sight of Paris restored my strength, and I ran the whole length of the alley I had so often walked.

That night no one was passing; it was like going through the midst of a dead city. The dawn began to break. When I reached the Rue d'Antin the great city stirred a little before quite awakening. Five o'clock struck at the church of Saint Roc at the moment when I entered Marguerite's house. I called out my name to the porter, who had had from me enough twenty-five franc pieces to know that I had a right to call on Mlle. Gautier at five in the morning. I passed without difficulty. I might have asked if Marguerite was at home, but he might have said 'No,' and I preferred to remain in doubt two minutes longer, for, as long as I doubted, there was hope.

I listened at the door, trying to discover a sound, a movement. Nothing. The silence of the country seemed to be continued here. I opened the door and entered. All the curtains were hermetically closed. I drew those of the dining-room and went towards the bedroom and pushed open the door. I sprang at the curtain cord and drew it violently. The curtain opened, a faint light made its way in. I rushed to the bed. It was empty.

I opened the doors one after another. I visited every room. No one. It was enough to drive one mad.

I went into the dressing-room, opened the window, and called Prudence several times. Mme. Duvernoy's window remained closed.

I went downstairs to the porter and asked him if Mlle. Gautier had come home during the day.

'Yes,' answered the man; 'with Mme. Duvernoy.'

'She left no word for me?'

'No.'

'Do you know what they did afterwards?'

'They went away in a carriage.'

'What sort of a carriage?'

'A private carriage.'

What could it all mean?

I rang at the next door.

'Where are you going sir?' asked the porter, when he had opened to me.

'To Mme. Duvernoy's.'

'She has not come back.'

'You are sure?'

'Yes, sir; here's a letter even, which was brought for her last night and which I have not yet given her.'

And the porter showed me a letter which I glanced at mechanically. I recognized Marguerite's writing. I took the letter. It was addressed, 'To Mme. Duvernoy, to forward to M. Duval.'

'This letter is for me,' I said to the porter, as I showed him the address.

'You are M. Duval?'

'Yes.'

'Ah! I remember. You often came to see Mme. Duvernoy.'

When I was in the street I broke the seal of the letter. If a thunder-bolt had fallen at my feet I should have been less startled than I was by what I read.

'By the time you read this letter, Armand, I shall be the mistress of another man. All is over between us.

'Go back to your father, my friend, and to your sister, and there, by the side of a pure young girl, ignorant of all our miseries, you will soon forget what you would have suffered through that lost creature who is called Marguerite Gautier, whom you have loved for an instant, and who owes to you the only happy moments of a life which, she hopes, will not be very long now.'

When I had read the last word, I thought I should have gone mad. For a moment I was really afraid of falling in the street. A cloud passed before my eyes and my blood beat in my temples. At last I came to myself a little. I looked about me, and was astonished to see the life of others continue without pausing at my distress.

I was not strong enough to endure the blow alone. Then I remembered that my father was in the same city, that I might be with him in ten minutes, and that, whatever might be the cause of my sorrow, he would share it.

I ran like a madman, like a thief, to the Hôtel de Paris; I found the key in the door of my father's room; I entered. He was reading. He showed so little astonishment at seeing me, that it was as if he was expecting me. I flung myself into his arms without saying a word. I gave him Marguerite's letter, and, falling on my knees beside his bed, I wept hot tears.

CHAPTER XXIII

When the current of life had resumed its course, I could not believe that the day which I saw dawning would not be like those which had preceeded it. There were moments when I fancied that some circumstance, which I could not recollect, had obliged me to spend the night away from Marguerite, but that, if I returned to Bougival, I should find her again as anxious as I had been, and that she would ask me what had detained me away from her so long.

When one's existence has contracted a habit, such as that of this love, it seems impossible that the habit should be broken without at the same time breaking all the other springs of life. I was forced from time to time to reread Marguerite's letter, in order to convince myself that I had not been dreaming.

My body, succumbing to the moral shock, was incapable of movement. Anxiety, the night walk, and the morning's news had prostrated me. My father profited by this total prostration of all my faculties to demand of me a formal promise to accompany him. I promised all that he asked, for I was incapable of sustaining a discussion, and I needed some affection to help me to live, after what had happened. I was too thankful that my father was willing to console me under such a calamity.

All that I remember is that on that day, about five o'clock, he took me with him in a hired carriage. Without a word to me, he had had my luggage packed and put up behind the carriage with his own, and so he carried me off. I did not realize what I was doing until the town had disappeared and the solitude of the road recalled to me the emptiness of my heart. Then my tears again began to flow.

My father had realized that words, even from him, would do nothing to console me, and he let me weep without saying a word, only sometimes pressing my hand, as if to remind me that I had a friend at my side.

At night I slept a little. I dreamed of Marguerite.

I woke with a start, not recalling why I was in the carriage. Then the truth came back upon me, and I let my head sink on my breast. I dared not say anything to my father. I was afraid he would say, 'You see I was right when I declared that this woman did not love you.' But he did not use his advantage, and we reached C. without his having said anything to me except to speak of matters quite apart from the event which had occasioned my leaving Paris.

When I embraced my sister, I remembered what Marguerite had said about her in her letter, and I saw at once how little my sister, good as she was, would be able to make me forget my mistress.

Shooting had begun, and my father thought that it would be a distraction for me. He got up shooting parties with friends and neighbours. I went without either reluctance or enthusiasm, with that sort of apathy into which I had sunk since my departure.

We were beating about for game and I was given my post. I put down my unloaded gun at my side, and meditated. I watched the clouds pass. I let my thoughts wander over the solitary plains, and from time to time I heard some one call to me and point to a hare not ten paces off.

None of these details escaped my father, and he was not deceived by my exterior calm. He was well aware that, broken as I now was, I should some day experience a terrible reaction, which might be dangerous, and, without seeming to make any effort to console me, he did his utmost to distract my thoughts.

My sister, naturally, knew nothing of what had happened, and she could not understand how it was that I, who had formerly been so light-hearted, had suddenly become so sad and dreamy.

Sometimes, surprising in the midst of my sadness my father's anxious scrutiny, I pressed his hand as if to ask him tacitly to forgive me for the pain which, in spite of myself, I was giving him.

Thus a month passed, but at the end of that time I could endure it no longer. The memory of Marguerite pursued me unceasingly. I had loved, I still loved this woman so much that

I could not suddenly become indifferent to her. I had to love or to hate her. Above all, whatever I felt for her, I had to see her again, and at once. This desire possessed my mind, and with all the violence of a will which had begun to reassert itself in a body so long inert.

It was not enough for me to see Marguerite in a month, a week. I had to see her the very next day after the day when the thought had occurred to me; and I went to my father and told him that I had been called to Paris on business, but that I should return promptly. No doubt he guessed the reason of my departure, for he insisted that I should stay, but, seeing that if I did not carry out my intention the consequences, in the state in which I was, might be fatal, he embraced me, and begged me, almost with tears, to return without delay.

I did not sleep on the way to Paris. Once there, what was I going to do? I did not know; I only knew that it must be something connected with Marguerite. I went to my rooms to change my clothes, and, as the weather was fine and it was still early, I made my way to the Champs-Élysées. At the end of half an hour I saw Marguerite's carriage, at some distance, coming from the Rond-Point to the Place de la Concorde. She had purchased her horses, for the carriage was just as I was accustomed to see it, but she was not in it. Scarcely had I noticed this fact, when looking around me, I saw Marguerite on foot, accompanied by a woman whom I had never seen.

As she passed me she turned pale, and a nervous smile tightened about her lips. For my part, my heart beat violently in my breast; but I succeeded in giving a cold expression to my face, as I bowed coldly to my former mistress, who just then reached her carriage, into which she got with her friend.

I knew Marguerite: this unexpected meeting must certainly upset her. No doubt she had heard that I had gone away, and had thus been reassured as to the consequences of our rupture; but, seeing me again in Paris, finding herself face to face with me, pale as I was, she must have realized that I had not returned without purpose, and she must have asked herself what the purpose was.

If I had seen Marguerite unhappy, if, in revenging myself upon her, I could have come to her aid, I should perhaps have forgiven her, and certainly I should have never dreamt of doing her an injury. But I found her apparently happy, some one else had restored to her the luxury I could not give her; her breaking with me seemed to assume a character of the basest self-interest; I was lowered in my own esteem as well as in my love. I resolved that she should pay for what I had suffered.

I could not be indifferent to what she did, consequently what would hurt her the most would be my indifference; it was, therefore, this sentiment which I must affect, not only in her eyes, but in the eyes of others.

I tried to put on a smiling countenance, and I went to call on Prudence. The maid announced me, and I had to wait a few minutes in the drawing-room. At last Mme. Duvernoy appeared and asked me into her boudoir; as I seated myself I heard the drawing-room door open, a light footstep made the floor creak and the front door was closed violently.

'I am disturbing you,' I said to Prudence.

'Not in the least. Marguerite was there. When she heard you announced she made her escape; it was she who has just gone out.'

'Is she afraid of me now?'

'No, but she is afraid that you would not wish to see her.'

'But why?' I said, drawing my breath with difficulty, for I was choked with emotion. 'The poor girl left me for her carriage, her furniture, and her diamonds; she did quite right, and I don't bear her any grudge. I met her today.' I continued carelessly.

'Where?' asked Prudence, looking at me and seeming to ask herself if this was the same man whom she had known so madly in love.

'In the Champs-Élysées. She was with another woman, very pretty. Who is she?'

'What was she like?'

'Blond, slender, with side curls; blue eyes; very elegant.'

'Ah! It was Olympe; she is really very pretty.'

'Whom does she live with?'

'With nobody; with anybody.'

'Where does she live?'

'Rue Tronchet, No.—. Do you want to make love to her?'

'One never knows.'

'And Marguerite?'

'I should hardly tell you the truth if I said I think no more about her; but I am one of those with whom everything depends on the way in which one breaks with them. Now Marguerite ended with me so lightly that I realize I was a great fool to have been as much in love with her as I was, for I was really very much in love with that girl.'

You can imagine the way in which I said that; the sweat broke out on my forehead.

'She was very fond of you, you know, and she still is; the proof is, that after meeting you today, she came straight to tell me about it. When she got here she was all of a tremble; I thought she was going to faint.'

'Well, what did she say?'

'She said, "He is sure to come here," and she begged me to ask you to forgive her.'

'I have forgiven her, you may tell her. She was a good girl; but, after all, like the others, and I ought to have expected what happened. I am even grateful to her, for I see now what would have happened if I had lived with her altogether. It was ridiculous.'

'She will be very glad to find that you take it so well. It was quite time she left you, my dear fellow. The rascal of an agent to whom she had offered to sell her furniture went around to her creditors to find out how much she owed; they took fright, and in two days she would have been sold up.'

'And now is it all paid?'

'More or less.'

'And who supplied the money?'

'The Comte de N. Ah, my dear friend, there are men made on purpose for such occasions. To cut a long story short he gave her twenty thousand francs, but he has had his way at last. He knows quite well that Marguerite is not in love with him; but he is very nice with her all the same. As you have seen, he has repurchased her horses, he had taken her jewels out of pawn, and he gives her as much money as the duke used to give her; if she likes to live quietly, he will stay with her a long time.'

'And what is she doing? Is she still living in Paris altogether?'

'She would never go back to Bougival after you went. I had to go myself and see after all her things, and yours, too. I made a package of them and you can send here for them. You will find everything, except a little case with your initials. Marguerite wanted to keep it. If you really want it, I will ask her for it.'

'Let her keep it,' I stammered, for I felt the tears rise from my heart to my eyes at the recollection of the village where I had been so happy, and at the thought that Marguerite cared to keep something which had belonged to me and would recall me to her. If she had entered at that moment my thoughts of vengeance would have disappeared, and I should have fallen at her feet.

'For the rest,' continued Prudence, 'I never saw her as she is now; she hardly takes any sleep, she goes to all the balls, she goes to suppers, she even drinks. The other day, after a supper, she had to stay in bed for a week; and when the doctor let her get up, she began again at the risk of her life. Shall you go and see her?'

'What is the good? I came to see you, because you have always been charming to me, and I knew you before I ever knew Marguerite. I owe it to you that I have been her lover, and also, don't I, that I am her lover no longer?'

'Well, I did all I could to get her away from you, and I believe you will be thankful to me later on.'

'I owe you a double gratitude,' I added, rising, for I was disgusted with the woman, seeing her take every word I said to her as if it were serious.

'You are going?'

'Yes.'

I had learned enough.

'When shall I be seeing you?'

'Soon. Good-bye.'

'Good-bye.'

Prudence saw me to the door, and I went back to my own rooms with tears of rage in my eyes and a desire for vengeance in my heart.

So Marguerite was no different from the others; so the steadfast love that she had had for me could not resist the desire of returning to her former life, and the need of having a carriage and plunging into dissipation. So I said to myself, as I lay awake at night, though if I had reflected as calmly as I professed to I should have seen in this new and turbulent life of Marguerite the attempt to silence a constant thought, a ceaseless memory. Unfortunately, evil passion had the upper hand, and I only sought for some means of avenging myself on the poor creature. Oh, how petty and vile is the man when he is wounded in one of his narrow passions!

This Olympe whom I had seen was, if not a friend of Marguerite, at all events the woman with whom she was most often seen since her return to Paris. She was going to give a ball, and, as I took it for granted that Marguerite would be there, I tried to get an invitation and succeeded.

When, full of my sorrowful emotions, I arrived at the ball, it was already very animated. They were dancing, shouting even, and in one of the quadrilles I perceived Marguerite dancing with the Comte de N., who seemed proud of showing her off, as if he said to everybody: 'This woman is mine.'

I leaned against the mantelpiece just opposite Marguerite and watched her dancing. Her face changed the moment she caught sight of me. I saluted her casually with a glance of the eyes and a wave of the hand.

When I reflected that after the ball she would go home, not with me but with that rich fool, when I thought of what would follow their return, the blood rose to my face, and I felt the need of doing something to trouble their relations.

After the dance I went up to the mistress of the house, who displayed for the benefit of her guests a dazzling bosom and magnificent shoulders. She was beautiful, and, from the point of view of figure, more beautiful than Marguerite. I realized this fact still more clearly from certain glances which Marguerite bestowed upon her while I was talking with her. The man who was the lover of such a woman might well be as proud of M. de N., and she was beautiful enough to inspire a passion not less great than that which Marguerite had inspired in me. At that moment she had no lover. It would not be difficult to become so; it depended only on showing enough money to attract her attention.

I made up my mind. That woman should be my mistress. I began by dancing with her. Half an hour afterward, Marguerite, pale as death, put on her wrap and left the ball.

CHAPTER XXIV

It was something already, but it was not enough. I saw the hold which I had upon this woman, and I took a cowardly advantage of it.

When I think that she is dead now, I ask myself if God will ever forgive me for the wrong I did her.

After the supper, which was noisy as could be, there was gambling. I sat by the side of Olympe and put down my money so recklessly that she could not but notice me. In an instant I had gained one hundred and fifty or two hundred louis, which I spread out before me on the table, and on which she fastened her eyes greedily.

I was the only one not too completely absorbed by the game, and able to pay her some attention. All the rest of the night I gained, and it was I who gave her money to play, for she had lost all she had before her and probably all she had in the house.

At five in the morning, the guests departed. I had gained three hundred louis.

All the players were already on their way down stairs; I was the only one who had remained behind, and as I did not know any of them, no one noticed it. Olympe herself was lighting the way, and I was going to follow the others, when, turning back, I said to her:

'I must speak to you.'

'Tomorrow,' she said.

'No, now.'

'What have you to say?'

'You will see.'

And I went back into the room.

'You have lost,' I said.

'Yes.'

'All that you had in the house?'

She hesitated.

'Be frank.'

'Well, it is true.'

'I have won three hundred louis. Here they are, if you will let me stay here tonight.'

And I threw the gold on the table.

'And why this proposition?'

'Because I am in love with you, of course.'

'No, but because you love Marguerite, and you want to have your revenge upon her by becoming my lover. You don't deceive a woman like me, my dear friend; unluckily, I am still too young and too good-looking to accept the part that you offer me.'

'So you refuse?'

'Yes.'

'Would you rather take me for nothing? It is I who wouldn't accept then. Think it over, my dear Olympe; if I had sent some one to offer you these three hundred louis on my behalf, on the conditions I attach to them, you would have accepted. I preferred to speak to you myself. Accept without inquiring into my reasons; say to yourself that you are beautiful, and that there is nothing surprising in my being in love with you.'

Marguerite was a woman in the same position as Olympe, and yet I should never have dared to say to her the first time I met her what I had said to the other woman. I loved Marguerite. I saw in her instincts which were lacking in the other, and at the very moment in which I made my bargain, I felt a disgust toward the woman with whom I was making it.

She accepted, of course, in the end, and at midday I left her house as her lover; but I quitted her without a recollection of the caresses and of the words of love which she had felt bound to shower upon me in return for the six thousand francs which I left with her. And yet there were men who had ruined themselves for that woman.

From that day I inflicted on Marguerite a continual persecution. Olympe and she gave up seeing one another, as you might imagine. I gave my new mistress a carriage and jewels. I gambled, I committed every extravagance which could be expected of a man in love with such a woman as Olympe. The report of my new infatuation was immediately spread abroad.

Prudence herself was taken in, and finally thought that I had completely forgotten Marguerite. Marguerite herself, whether she guessed my motive or was deceived like everybody else, preserved a perfect dignity in response to the insults which I heaped upon her daily. Only, she seemed to suffer, for whenever I met her she was more and more pale, more and more sad. My love for her, carried to the point at which it was transformed into hatred, rejoiced at the sight of her daily sorrow. Often, when my cruelty toward her became infamous, Marguerite lifted upon me such appealing eyes that I blushed for the part I was playing, and was ready to implore her forgiveness.

But my repentance was only of a moment's duration, and Olympe, who had finally put aside all self-respect, and discovered that by annoying Marguerite she could get from me whatever she wanted, constantly stirred up my resentment against her, and insulted her whenever she found an opportunity, with the cowardly persistence of a woman licensed by the authority of a man.

At last Marguerite gave up going to balls or theatres, for fear of meeting Olympe and me. Then direct impertinences gave way to anonymous letters, and there was not a shameful thing which I did not encourage my mistress to relate and which I did not myself relate in reference to Marguerite.

To reach such a point I must have been literally mad. I was like a man drunk upon bad wine, who falls into one of those nervous exaltations in which the hand is capable of committing a crime without the head knowing anything about it. In the midst of it all I endured a martyrdom. The not disdainful calm, the not contemptuous dignity with which Marguerite responded to all my attacks, and which raised her above me in my own eyes, enraged me still more against her.

One evening Olympe had gone somewhere or other, and had met Marguerite, who for once had not spared the foolish creature, so that she had to retire in confusion. Olympe returned in a fury, and Marguerite fainted and had to be carried out. Olympe related to me what had happened, declared that Marguerite, seeing her alone, had revenged herself upon her because she was my mistress, and that I must write and tell her to respect the woman whom I loved, whether I was present or absent.

I need not tell you that I consented, and that I put into the letter which I sent to her address, the same day, everything bitter, shameful and cruel that I could think of.

This time the blow was more than the unhappy creature could endure without replying. I felt sure that an answer would come, and I resolved not to go out all day. About two there was a ring, and Prudence entered.

I tried to assume an indifferent air as I asked her what had brought her; but that day Mme. Duvernoy was not in a laughing humour, and in a really moved voice she said to me that since my return, that is to say for about three weeks, I had left no occasion untried which could give pain to Marguerite, that she was completely upset by it, and that the scene of last night and my angry letter of the morning had forced her to take to her bed. In short, without making any reproach, Marguerite sent to ask me for a little pity, since she had no longer the moral or physical strength to endure what I was making her suffer.

'That Mlle. Gautier,' I said to Prudence, 'should turn me out of her own house is quite reasonable, but that she should insult the woman whom I love, under the pretence that this woman is my mistress, is a thing I will never permit.'

'My friend,' said Prudence, 'you are under the influence of a woman who has neither heart nor sense; you are in love with her, it is true, but that is not a reason for torturing a woman who can not defend herself.'

'Let Mlle. Gautier send me her Comte de N. and the sides will be equal.'

'You know very well that she will not do that. So, my dear Armand, let her alone. If you saw her you would be ashamed of the way in which you are treating her. She is white, she coughs – she won't last long now.'

And Prudence held out her hand to me, adding:

'Come and see her; it will make her very happy.'

'I have no desire to meet M. de N.'

'M. de N. is never there. She can not endure him.'

'If Marguerite wished to see me, she knows where I live; let her come to see me, but for my part, I will never put foot in the Rue d'Antin.'

'Will you receive her well?'

'Certainly.'

'Well, I am sure that she will come.'

'Let her come.'

'Shall you be out today?'

'I shall be at home all evening.'

'I will tell her.'

And Prudence left me.

I did not even write to tell Olympe not to expect me. I never troubled much about her, scarcely going to see her one night a week. She consoled herself, I believe, with an actor from some theatre or other.

I went out for dinner and came back almost immediately. I had a fire lit in my room and I told Joseph he could go out.

I can give you no idea of the different impressions which agitated me during the hour in which I waited; but when, toward nine o'clock, I heard a ring, they thronged together into one such emotion, that, as I opened the door, I was obliged to lean against the wall to keep myself from falling.

Fortunately the anteroom was in half darkness, and the change in my countenance was less visible.

Marguerite entered.

She was dressed in black and veiled. I could scarcely recognize her face through the veil. She went into the drawing-room and raised her veil. She was as pale as marble.

'I am here, Armand,' she said; 'you wished to see me and I have come.'

And letting her head fall on her hands, she burst into tears.

I went up to her.

'What is the matter?' I said to her in a low voice.

She pressed my hand without a word, for tears still veiled her voice. But after a few minutes, recovering herself a little, she said to me:

'You have been very unkind to me, Armand, and I have done nothing to you.'

'Nothing?' I answered, with a bitter smile.

'Nothing but what circumstances forced me to do.'

I do not know if you have ever in your life experienced, or if you will ever experience, what I felt at the sight of Marguerite.

The last time she had come to see me she had sat in the same place where she was now sitting; only, since then, she had been the mistress of another man, other kisses than mine had touched her lips, toward which, in spite of myself, my own reached out, and yet I felt that I loved this woman as much, more perhaps, than I had ever loved her.

It was difficult for me to begin the conversation on the subject which brought her. Marguerite no doubt realized it, for she went on:

'I have come to trouble you, Armand, for I have two things to ask: pardon for what I said yesterday to Mlle. Olympe, and pity for what you are perhaps still ready to do to me. Intentionally or not, since your return you have given me so much pain that I should be incapable now of enduring a fourth part of what I have endured till now. You will have pity on me, won't you? And you will understand that a man who is not heartless has other nobler things to do than to take his revenge upon a sick and sad woman like me. See, take my hand. I am in a fever. I left my bed to come to you, and ask, not your friendship, but for your indifference.'

I took Marguerite's hand. It was burning, and the poor woman shivered under her fur cloak.

I rolled the arm-chair in which she was sitting up to the fire.

'Do you think, then, that I did not suffer,' said I 'on that night when, after waiting for you in the country, I came to look for you in Paris, and found nothing but the letter which nearly drove me mad? How could you have deceived me, Marguerite, when I loved you so much?'

'Do not speak of that Armand; I did not come to speak of that. I wanted to see you only not an enemy, and I wanted to take your hand once more. You have a mistress; she is young, pretty, you love her they say. Be happy with her and forget me.'

'And you. You are happy, no doubt?'

'Have I the face of a happy woman, Armand? Do not mock my sorrow, you, who know better than any one what its cause and its depth are.'

'It only depended on you not to have been unhappy at all, if you are as you say.'

'No, my friend; circumstances were stronger than my will.
I obeyed, not the instincts of a light woman, as you seem to
say, but a serious necessity, and reasons which you will know
one day, and which will make you forgive me.'

'Why do you not tell me those reasons today?'

'Because they would bring about an impossible reunion
between us, and they would separate you perhaps from those
from whom you must not be separated.'

'Who do you mean?'

'I can not tell you.'

'Then you are lying to me.'

Marguerite rose and went toward the door. I could not
behold this silent and expressive sorrow without being
touched, when I compared in my mind this pale and weeping
woman with the madcap who had made fun of me at the
Opéra Comique.

'You shall not go,' I said, putting myself in front of the
door.

'Why?'

'Because, in spite of what you have done to me, I love you
always, and I want you to stay here.'

'To turn me out tomorrow? No; it is impossible. Our
destinies are separate; do not try to reunite them. You will
despise me perhaps, while now you can only hate me.'

'No, Marguerite,' I cried, feeling all my love and all my
desire reawaken at the contact of this woman. 'No, I will
forget everything, and we will be happy as we promised one
another that we would be.'

Marguerite shook her head doubtfully, and said:

'Am I not your slave, your dog? Do with me what you will.
Take me; I am yours.'

And throwing off her cloak and hat, she flung them on the
sofa, and began hurriedly to undo the front of her dress, for,
by one of those reactions so frequent in her malady, the blood
rushed to her head and stifled her. A hard, dry cough
followed.

'Tell my coachman,' she said, 'to go back with the carriage.'

I went down myself and sent him away. When I returned
Marguerite was lying in front of the fire, and her teeth
chattered with cold.

I took her in my arms. I undressed her, without her making a movement, and carried her, icy cold, to the bed. Then I sat beside her and tried to warm her with my caresses. She did not speak a word, but smiled at me.

It was a strange night. All Marguerite's life seemed to have passed into the kisses with which she covered me, and I loved her so much that in my transports of feverish love I asked myself whether I should not kill her, so that she might never belong to another.

A month of love like that, and there would have remained only the corpse of heart or body.

The dawn found us both awake. Marguerite was livid white, She did not speak a word. From time to time, big tears rolled from her eyes, and stayed upon her cheeks, shining like diamonds. Her thin arms opened, from time to time, to hold me fast, and fell back helplessly on the bed.

For a moment it seemed to me as if I could forget all that had passed since I had left Bougival and I said to Marguerite:

'Shall we go away and leave Paris?'

'No, no!' she cried, almost with affright; 'we should be too unhappy. I can do no more to make you happy, but while there is a breath of life in me, I will be the slave of your fancies. At whatever hour of the day or night you will, come, and I will be yours; but do not link your future any more with mine, you would be too unhappy and you would make me too unhappy. I shall still be pretty for a while; make the most of it, but ask nothing more.'

When she had gone, I was frightened at the solitude in which she had left me. Two hours afterward I was still sitting on the side of the bed, looking at the pillow which kept the imprint of her form, and asking myself what was to become of me, between my love and my jealousy.

At five o'clock, without knowing what I was going to do, I went to the Rue d'Antin.

Nanine opened the door to me.

'Madame can not receive you,' she said in an embarrassed way.

'Why?'

'Because M. le Comte de N. is there, and he has given orders to let no one in.'

'Quite so,' I stammered; 'I forgot.'

I went home like a drunken man, and do you know what I did during the moment of jealous delirium which was long enough for the shameful thing I was going to do? I said to myself that the woman was laughing at me; I saw her alone with the count, saying over to him the same words that she had said to me in the night, and taking a five-hundred-franc note, I sent it to her with these words:

'You went away so suddenly that I forgot to pay you. Here is the price of your night.'

Then when the letter was sent I went out as if to free myself from the instantaneous remorse of this infamous action.

I went to see Olympe, whom I found trying on dresses, and when we were alone she sang obscene songs to amuse me. She was the very type of the shameless, heartless, senseless courtesan, for me at least, for perhaps some men might have dreamed of her as I dreamed of Marguerite. She asked me for money. I gave it to her, and, free then to go, I returned home.

Marguerite had not answered.

I need not tell you in what state of agitation I spent the next day. At half past nine a messenger brought me an envelope containing my letter and the five-hundred-franc note, not a word more.

'Who gave you this?'

'A lady who was starting with her maid in the next mail for Boulogne, and who told me not to take it until the coach was out of the courtyard.'

I rushed to the Rue d'Antin.

'Madame left for England at six o'clock,' said the porter.

There was nothing to hold me in Paris any longer, neither hate nor love. I was exhausted by this series of shocks. One of my friends was setting out on a tour of the East. I told my father I should like to accompany him; my father gave me drafts and letters of introductions, and eight or ten days afterward I embarked at Marseilles.

It was at Alexandria that I learned from an *attaché* at the embassy, whom I had sometimes seen at Marguerite's, that the poor girl was seriously ill.

I then wrote her the letter which she answered in the way you know; I received it at Toulon.

I started at once, and you know the rest.

Now you have only to read a few sheets which Julie Duprat gave me; they are the best commentary on what I have just told you.

CHAPTER XXV

Armand, tired by this long narrative, often interrupted by his tears, put his two hands over his forehead and closed his eyes to think, or to try to sleep, after giving me the pages written by the hand of Marguerite. A few minutes after, a more rapid breathing told me that Armand slept, but that light sleep which the least sound banishes.

This is what I read; I copy it without adding or omitting a syllable:

Today is the 15th of December. I have been ill three or four days. This morning I stayed in bed. The weather is dark, I am sad; there is no one by me. I think of you, Armand. And you, where are you, while I write these lines? Far from Paris, far, far, they tell me, and perhaps you have already forgotten Marguerite. Well, be happy; I owe you the only happy moments of my life.

I can not help wanting to explain all my conduct to you, and I have written you a letter; but, written by a girl like me, such a letter might seem to be a lie, unless death had sanctified it by its authority, and, instead of a letter, it were a confession.

Today I am ill; I may die of this illness, for I have always had the presentiment that I shall die young. My mother died of consumption, and the way I have always lived could but increase the only heritage she ever left me. But I do not want to die without clearing up for you everything about me; that is, if, when you come back, you will still trouble yourself about the poor girl whom you loved before you went away.

This is what the letter contained; I shall like writing it over again, so as to give myself another proof of my own justification.

You remember, Armand, how the arrival of your father surprised us at Bougival; you remember the involuntary fright that his arrival caused me, and the scene which took place between you and him, which you told me of in the evening.

Next day, when you were in Paris, waiting for your father, and he did not return, a man came to the door and handed in a letter from M. Duval.

His letter, which I inclose with this, begged me, in the most serious terms, to keep you away on the following day, on some excuse or other, and to see your father, who wished to speak to me, and asked me particularly not to say anything to you about it.

You know how I insisted on your returning to Paris next day.

You had only been gone an hour when your father presented himself. I won't say what impression his severe face made upon me. Your father had the old theory that a courtesan is a being without heart or reason, a sort of machine for coining gold, always ready, like the machine, to bruise the hand that gives her everything, and to tear in pieces, without pity or discernment, those who set her in motion.

Your father had written me a very polite letter, in order that I might consent to see him; he did not present himself quite as he had written. His manner at first was so stiff, insolent, and even threatening, that I had to make him understand that I was in my own house, and that I had no need to render him an account of my life, except because of the sincere affection which I had for his son.

M. Duval calmed down a little, but still went on to say that he could not any longer allow his son to ruin himself over me; that I was beautiful, it was true, but, however beautiful I might be, I ought not to make use of my beauty to spoil the future of a young man by such expenditure as I was causing.

At that there was only one thing to do, to show him the proof that since I was your mistress I had spared no sacrifice to be faithful to you without asking for more money than you had to give me. I showed him the pawn tickets, the receipts of the people to whom I had sold what I could not pawn; I told him of my resolve to part with my furniture in order to pay my debts, and live with you without being a too heavy expense. I told him of our happiness, of how you had shown me the possibility of a quieter and happier life, and he ended by giving in to the evidence, offering me his hand, and asking pardon for the way in which he had at first approached me.

Then he said to me:

'So, madame, it is not by remonstrances or by threats, but by entreaties, that I must endeavour to obtain from you a greater sacrifice than you have yet made for my son.'

I trembled at this beginning.

Your father came over to me, took both my hands, and continued in an affectionate voice:

'My child, do not take what I have to say to you amiss; only remember that there are sometimes in life cruel necessities for the heart, but that they must be submitted to. You are good, your soul has generosity unknown to many women who perhaps despise you, and are less worthy than you. But remember that there is not only the mistress, but the family; that besides love there are duties; that to the age of passion succeeds the age when man, if he is to be respected, must plant himself solidly in a serious position. My son has no fortune, and yet he is ready to abandon to you the legacy of his mother. If he accepted from you the sacrifice which you are on the point of making, his honour and dignity would require him to give you, in exchange for it, this income, which would always put you out of danger of adversity. But he can not accept this sacrifice, because the world, which does not know you, would give a wrong interpretation to this acceptance, and such an interpretation must not tarnish the name which we bear. No one would consider whether Armand loves you, whether you loved him, whether this mutual love means happiness to him and redemption to you; they would see only one thing, that Armand Duval allowed a kept woman (forgive me, my child, for what I am forced to say to you) to sell all she had for him. Then the day of reproaches and regrets would arrive, be sure, for you or for others, and you would both bear a chain that you could not sever. What would you do then? Your youth would be lost, my son's future destroyed; and I, his father, should receive from only one of my children the recompense that I look for from both of them.

'You are young, beautiful, life will console you; you are noble, and the memory of a good deed will redeem you from many past deeds. During the six months that he has known you Armand has forgotten me. I wrote to him four times, and he has never once replied. I might have died and he not known it!

'Whatever may be your resolution of living otherwise than as you have lived, Armand, who loves you, will never consent to the seclusion to which his modest fortune would condemn you, and to which your beauty does not entitle you. Who knows what he would do then! He has gambled, I know; without telling you of it, I know also, but, in a moment of madness, he might have lost part of what I have saved, during many years, for my daughter's portion, for him, and for the repose of my old age. What might have happened may yet happen.

'Are you sure, besides, that the life which you are giving up for him will never again come to attract you? Are you sure, you who have loved him, that you will never love another? Would you not suffer on seeing the hindrances set by your love to your lover's life, hindrances for which you would be powerless to console him, if, with age, thoughts of ambition should succeed to dreams of love? Think over all that, madame. You love Armand; prove it to him by the sole means which remains to you of yet proving it to him, by sacrificing your love to his future. No misfortune has yet arrived, but one will arrive, and perhaps a greater one than those which I foresee. Armand might become jealous of a man who has loved you; he might provoke him, fight, be killed. Think, then, what you would suffer in the presence of a father who should call on you to render an account for the life of his son!

'Finally, my dear child, let me tell you all, for I have not yet told you all, let me tell you what has brought me to Paris. I have a daughter, as I have told you, young, beautiful, pure as an angel. She loves, and she, too, has made this love the dream of her life. I wrote all that to Armand, but, absorbed in you, he made no reply. Well, my daughter is about to marry. She is to marry the man whom she loves; she enters an honourable family, which requires that mine has to be no less honourable. The family of the man who is to become my son-in-law has learned what manner of life Armand is leading in Paris, and had declared to me that the marriage must be broken off if

Armand continues this life. The future of a child who has done nothing against you, and who has the right of looking forward to a happy future, is in your hands. Have you the right, have you the strength, to shatter it? In the name of your love and of your repentance, Marguerite, grant me the happiness of my child.'

I wept silently, my friend, at all these reflections which I had so often made, and which, in the mouth of your father, took a yet more serious reality. I said to myself all that your father dared not say to me, though it had come to his lips twenty times; that I was, after all, only a kept woman, and that whatever excuse I gave to our *liaison*, it would always look like calculation on my part; that my past life left me no right to dream of such a future, and that I was accepting responsibilities for which my habits and reputation were far from giving any guarantee. In short, I loved you, Armand.

The paternal way in which M. Duval had spoken to me; the pure memories that he awakened in me; the respect of this old man, which I would gain; yours, which I was sure of gaining later on: all that called up in my heart thoughts which raised me in my own eyes with a sort of holy pride, unknown till then. When I thought that one day this old man, who was imploring me for the future of his son, would bid his daughter mingle my name with her prayers, as the name of a mysterious friend, I seemed to become transformed, and I felt a pride in myself.

The exultations of the moment perhaps exaggerated the truth of these impressions, but that was what I felt, friend, and these new feelings silenced the memory of the happy days I had spent with you.

'Tell me, sir,' I said to your father, wiping away my tears, 'do you believe that I love your son?'

'Yes,' said M. Duval.

'With a disinterested love?'

'Yes.'

'Do you believe that I had made this love the hope, the dream, the forgiveness of my life?'

'Implicitly.'

'Well, sir, embrace me once, as you would embrace your daughter, and I swear to you that that kiss, the only chaste kiss

I have ever had, will make me strong against my love, and that within a week your son will be once more at your side, perhaps unhappy for a time, but cured forever.'

'You are a noble child,' replied your father, kissing me on the forehead, 'and you are making an attempt for which God will reward you; but I greatly fear that you will have no influence upon my son.'

'Oh, be at rest, sir; he will hate me.'

I had to set up between us, as much for me as for you, an insurmountable barrier.

I wrote to Prudence to say that I accepted the proposition of the Comte de N., and that she was to tell him that I would sup with her and him. I sealed the letter, and, without telling what it contained, asked your father to have it forwarded to its address on reaching Paris.

He inquired of me what it contained.

'Your son's welfare,' I answered.

Your father embraced me once more. I felt two grateful tears on my forehead, like the baptism of my past faults, and at the moment when I consented to give myself up to another man I glowed with pride at the thought of what I was redeeming by this new fault.

It was quite natural, Armand. You told me that your father was the most honest man in the world.

M. Duval returned to his carriage, and set out for Paris.

I was only a woman, and when I saw you again I could not help weeping, but I did not give way.

Did I do right? That is what I ask myself today, as I lie ill in my bed, that I shall never leave, perhaps, until I am dead.

You are witness of what I felt as the hour of our separation approached; your father was no longer there to support me, and there was a moment when I was on the point of confessing everything to you, so terrified was I at the idea that you were going to hate and despise me.

One thing which you will not believe, perhaps, Armand, is that I prayed to God to give me strength; and what proves that he accepted my sacrifice is that he gave me the strength for which I prayed.

At supper I still had need of aid, for I could not think of what I was going to do, so much did I fear that my courage would fail me. Who would ever have said that I, Marguerite Gautier, would have suffered so at the mere thought of a new lover? I drank for forgetfulness, and when I woke next day I was beside the count.

That is the whole truth, friend. Judge me and pardon me, as I have pardoned you all the wrong that you have done me since that day.

CHAPTER XXVI

What followed that fatal night (Marguerite wrote) you know as well as I; but what you can not know, what you can not suspect, is what I have suffered since our separation.

I heard that your father had taken you away with him, but I felt sure that you could not live away from me for long, and when I met you in the Champs-Élysées, I was a little upset, but by no means surprised.

Then began that series of days; each of them brought me a fresh insult from you. I received them all with a kind of joy, for, besides proving to me that you still loved me, it seemed to me as if the more you persecuted me the more I should be raised in your eyes when you came to know the truth.

Do not wonder at my joy in martyrdom, Armand; your love for me has opened my heart to noble enthusiasm.

Still, I was not so strong as that all at once.

Between the time of the sacrifice made for you and the time of your return a long while elapsed, during which I was obliged to have recourse to physical means in order not to go mad, and in order to be blinded and deafened in the whirl of life into which I flung myself. Prudence has told you (has she not?) how I went to all the fêtes and balls and orgies. I had a sort of hope that I should kill myself by all these excesses, and I think it will not be long before this hope is realized. My health naturally got worse and worse, and when I sent Mme. Duvernoy to ask you for pity I was utterly worn out, body and soul.

I will not remind you, Armand, of the return you made for the last proof of love that I gave you, and of the outrage by which you drove away a dying woman, who could not resist your voice when you asked her for a night of love, and who, like a fool, thought for one instant, that she might again unite the past with the present. You had the right to do what you did, Armand; people have not always put so high a price on a night of mine!

I left everything after that. Olympe has my place with the Comte de N., and has told him, I hear, the reasons for my leaving him. The Comte de G. was at London. He is one of those men who give just enough importance to making love to women like me for it to be an agreeable pastime, and who are thus able to remain friends with women, not hating them because thay have never been jealous of them, and he is, too, one of those grand seigneurs who open only a part of their hearts to us, but the whole of their purses. It was of him that I immediately thought. I joined him in London. He received me as kindly as possible, but he was the lover there of a woman in society, and he feared to compromise himself if he were seen with me. He introduced me to his friends, who gave a supper in my honour, after which one of them took me home with him.

What else was there for me to do, my friend? If I had killed myself it would have burdened your life, which ought to be happy, with a needless remorse; and then, what is the good of killing oneself when one is so near dying already?

I became a body without a soul, a thing without a thought; I lived for some time in that automatic way; then I returned to Paris, and asked after you; I heard then that you were gone on a long voyage. There was nothing left to hold me to life. My existence became what it had been two years before I knew you. I tried to win back the duke, but I had offended him too deeply. Old men are not patient, no doubt because they realize that they are not eternal. I got weaker every day. I was pale and sad and thinner than ever. Men who buy love examine the goods before taking them. In Paris there were women in better health and not so thin as I was; I was rather forgotten. That is all the past up to yesterday.

Now I am seriously ill. I have written to the duke to ask him for money, for I have none, and the creditors have returned, and come to me with their bills with pitiless perseverance. Will the duke answer? Why are you not in Paris, Armand? You would come and see me, and your visits would do me good.

December 20.

The weather is horrible; it is snowing, and I am alone. I have been in such a fever for the last three days that I could not write you a word. No news, my friend; every day I hope vaguely for a letter from you, but it does not come, and no doubt it will never come. Only men are strong enough not to forgive. The duke has not answered.

Prudence is pawning my things again.

I have been spitting blood all the time. Oh, you would be sorry for me if you could see me. You are indeed happy to be under a warm sky, and not, like me, with a whole winter of ice on your chest. Today I got up for a little while, and watched the life of Paris passing below, the life with which I have now nothing more to do. I saw the faces of some people I knew, passing rapidly, joyous and careless. Not one lifted his eyes to my window. However, a few young men have come to inquire for me. Once before I was ill, and you, though you did not know me, though you had had nothing from me but an impertinence the day I met you first, you came to inquire after me every day. We spent six months together. I had all the love for you that a woman's heart can hold and give, and you are far away, you are cursing me, and there is not a word of consolation from you. But it is only chance that has made you leave me, I am sure, for if you were in Paris, you would not leave my bedside.

December 25.

My doctor tells me I must not write every day. And indeed my memories only increase my fever, but yesterday I received a letter which did me good, more because of what it said than by the material help which it contained. I can write to you, then, today. This letter is from your father, and this is what it says:

'MADAME: I have just learned that you are ill. If I were in Paris I would come and ask after you myself; if my son were here I would send him; but I can not leave now, and Armand is six or seven hundred miles from here, permit me, then, simply to write to you, madame, to tell you how pained I am to hear of your illness, and believe in my sincere wishes for your speedy recovery.

'One of my good friends, M.H., will call on you; will you kindly receive him? I have intrusted him with a commission, the result of which I await impatiently.

'Believe me, madame,

'Yours most faithfully.'

This is the letter he sent me. Your father has a noble heart; love him well, my friend, for there are few men so worthy of being loved. This paper signed by his name has done me more good than all the prescriptions of our great doctor.

This morning M.H. called. He seemed much embarrassed by the delicate mission which M. Duval had entrusted to him. As a matter of fact, he came to bring me three thousand francs from your father. I wanted to refuse at first, but M.H. told me that my refusal would annoy M. Duval, who had authorized him to give me this sum now, and later on whatever I might need. I accepted it, for, coming from your father, it could not be exactly accepting alms. If I am dead when you come back, show your father what I have written for him, and tell him that in writing these lines the poor woman to whom he was kind enough to write so consoling a letter wept tears of gratitude and prayed God for him.

January 4.

I have passed some terrible days. I never knew the body could suffer so. Oh, my past life! I pay doubly for it now.

There has been some one to watch by me every night. I can not breathe. What remains of my poor existence is shared between being delirious and coughing.

The dining-room is full of sweets and all sorts of presents that my friends have brought. Some of them, I dare say, are hoping I shall be their mistress later on. If they could see what sickness has made of me, they would go away in terror.

Prudence is giving her New Year's presents with those I have received.

There is a thaw, and the doctor says that I may go out in a few days if the fine weather continues.

January 8.

I went out yesterday in my carriage. The weather was lovely. The Champs-Élysées was full of people. It was like the first smile of spring. Everything about me had a festive air. I never knew before that a ray of sunshine could contain so much joy, sweetness and consolation.

I met almost all the people I knew, all happy, all absorbed in their pleasures. How many happy people don't even know that they are happy! Olympe passed me in an elegant carriage that M. de N. has given her. She tried to insult me by her look. She little knows how far I am from such things now. A nice fellow, whom I have known for a long time, asked me if I would have supper with him and one of his friends, who, he said, was very anxious to make my acquaintance. I smiled sadly and gave him my hand, burning with fever. I never saw such an astonished countenance.

I came in at four, and had quite an appetite for my dinner. Going out has done me good. If I were only going to get well! How the sight of the life and happiness of others gives a desire of life to those who, only the night before, in the solitude of their souls and in the shadow of their sick-room only wanted to die soon!

January 10.

The hope of getting better was only a dream. I am back in bed again, covered with plasters that burn me. If I were to offer the body that people paid so dear for once, how much would they give, I wonder, today?

We must have done something very wicked before we were born, or else we must be going to be very happy indeed when we are dead, for God to let this life have all the tortures of expiation and all the sorrows of an ordeal.

January 12.

I am always ill.

The Comte de N. sent me some money yesterday. I did not keep it. I won't take anything from that man. It is through him that you are not here.

Oh, that good time at Bougival! Where is it now?

If I come out of this room alive I will make a pilgrimage to the house we lived in together, but I will never leave it until I am dead.

Who knows if I shall write to you tomorrow?

January 25.

I have not slept for eleven nights. I am suffocated. I imagine every moment that I am going to die. The doctor has forbidden me to touch a pen. Julie Duprat, who is looking after me, lets me write these few lines to you. Will you come back before I die? Is it all over between us forever? It seems to me as if I should get well if you come. What would be the good of getting well?

January 28.

This morning I was awakened by a great noise. Julie, who slept in my room, ran into the dining-room. I heard men's voices, and hers protesting against them in vain. She came back crying.

They had come to seize my things. I told her to let what they call justice have its way. The bailiff came into my room with his hat on. He opened the drawers, wrote down what he saw, and did not even seem to be aware that there was a dying woman in the bed that fortunately the charity of the law leaves me.

He said, indeed, before going, that I could appeal within nine days, but he left a man behind to keep watch. My God! what is to become of me? This scene has made me worse than I was before. Prudence wanted to go and ask your father's friend for money, but I would not let her.

I received your letter this morning. I was in need of it. Will my answer reach you in time? Will you ever see me again? This is a happy day, and it has made me forget all the days I have passed for the last six weeks. I seem as if I am better, in spite of the feeling of sadness under the impression of which I replied to you.

After all, no one is unhappy always.

When I think that it may happen to me not to die, for you to come back, for me to see the spring again, for you still to love me, and for us to begin over again our last year's life!

Fool that I am! I can scarcely hold the pen with which I write to you of this wild dream of my heart.

Whatever happens, I loved you well, Armand, and I would have died long ago if I had not had the memory of your love to help me and a sort of vague hope of seeing you beside me again.

February 4.

The Comte de G. has returned. His mistress has been unfaithful to him. He is very sad; he was very fond of her. He came to tell me all about it. The poor fellow is in rather a bad way as to money, all the same, he has paid my bailiff and sent away the man.

I talked to him about you, and he promised to tell you about me. I forgot that I had been his mistress, and he tried to make me forget it, too. He is a good friend.

The duke sent yesterday to inquire after me, and this morning he came to see me. I do not know how the old man still keeps alive. He remained with me three hours and did not say twenty words. Two big tears fell from his eyes when he saw how pale I was. The memory of his daughter's death made him weep, no doubt. He will have seen her die twice. His back was bowed, his head bent toward the ground, his lips drooping, his eyes vacant. Age and sorrow weigh with a double weight on his worn-out body. He did not reproach me. It looks as if he rejoiced secretly to see the ravages that disease had made in me. He seemed proud of being still on his feet, while I, who am still young, was broken down by suffering.

The bad weather has returned. No one comes to see me. Julie watches by me as much as she can. Prudence, to whom I can no longer give as much as I used to, begins to make excuses for not coming.

Now that I am so near death, in spite of what the doctors tell me, for I have several, which proves that I am getting worse, I am almost sorry that I listened to your father; if I had known that I should only be taking a year of your future, I could not have resisted the longing to spend that year with you, and, at least, I should have died with a friend to hold my hand. It is true that if we had lived together this year, I should not have died so soon.

God's will be done!

February 5.

Oh, come, come, Armand! I suffer horribly; I am going to die, O God! I was so miserable yesterday that I wanted to spend the evening, which seemed as if it were going to be as long as the last anywhere but home. The duke came in the morning. It seems to me as if the sight of this old man, whom death has forgotten, makes me die faster.

Despite the burning fever which devoured me, I made them

dress me and take me to the Vaudeville. Julie put on some rouge for me, without which I should have looked like a corpse. I had the box where I gave you our first rendezvous. All the time I had my eyes fixed on the stall where you sat that day, though a sort of country fellow sat there, laughing loudly at all the foolish things that the actors said. I was half dead when they brought me home. I coughed and spat blood all the night. Today I can not speak, I can scarcely move my arm. My God! My God! I am going to die! I have been expecting it, but I can not get used to the thought of suffering more than I suffer now, and if —

After this the characters traced by Marguerite were indecipherable, and what followed was written by Julie Duprat.

February 18.

MONSIEUR ARMAND:

Since the day that Marguerite insisted on going to the theatre she has got worse and worse. She has completely lost her voice, and now the use of her limbs. What our poor friend suffers is impossible to say. I am not used to emotions of this kind, and I am in a state of constant fright.

How I wish you were here! She is almost always delirious; but delirious or lucid, it is always your name she pronounces, when she can speak a word.

The doctor tells me that she is not here for long. Since she got so ill the duke has not returned. He told the doctor that the sight was too much for him.

Mme. Duvernoy is not behaving well. This woman, who thought she could get more money out of Marguerite, at whose expense she was living almost completely, and contracted liabilities which she can not meet, and seeing that her neighbour is no longer of use to her, she does not even come to see her. Everybody is abandoning her. M. de G., prosecuted for his debts, has had to return to London. On leaving, he sent us more money; he has done all he could, but they have returned to seize the things, and the creditors are only waiting for her to die in order to sell everything.

I wanted to use my last resources to put a stop to it, but the bailiff told me it was no use, and that there are other seizures to follow. Since she must die, it is better to let everything go than to save it for her family, whom she never cared to see, and who have never cared for her. You can not conceive in the midst of what gilded misery the poor thing is dying. Yesterday we had absolutely no money. Plate, jewels, shawls, everything is in pawn; the rest sold or seized. Marguerite is still conscious of what goes on around her, and she suffers in body, mind and heart. Big tears trickle down her cheeks so thin and pale that you would never recognize the face of her whom you loved so much, if you could see her. She has made me promise to write to you when she can no longer write, and I write before her. She turns her eyes toward me, but she no longer sees me; her eyes are already veiled by the coming of death; yet she smiles, and all her thoughts, all her soul are yours, I am sure.

Every time the door opens her eyes brighten, and she thinks you are going to come in; when she sees that it is not you, her face resumes its sorrowful expression, a cold sweat breaks out over it, and her cheek-bones flush.

February 19, *midnight.*

What a sad day we have had today, poor M. Armand! This morning Marguerite was stifling; the doctor bled her, and her voice returned to her for a while. The doctor begged her to see a priest. She said 'Yes' and he went himself to fetch an *abbé* from Saint Roch.

Meanwhile Marguerite called me up to her bed, asked me to open a cupboard, and pointed out a cap and a long chemise covered with lace, and said in a feeble voice:

'I shall die as soon as I have confessed. Then you will dress me in these things; it is the whim of a dying woman.'

Then she embraced me with tears and added:

'I can speak, but I am stifled when I speak; I am stifling. Air!'

I burst into tears, opened the window, and a few minutes afterward the priest entered. I went to him; when he knew where he was, he seemed afraid of being badly received.

'Come in boldly, father,' I said to him.

He stayed a very short time in the room, and when he came out he said to me:

'She lived a sinner, and she will die a Christian.'

A few minutes afterward he returned with a choir boy bearing a crucifix, and a sacristan who went before them ringing the bell to announce that God was coming to the dying one.

They went all three into the bedroom where so many strange words have been said, but was now a sort of holy tabernacle.

I fell on my knees. I do not know how long the impression of what I saw will last, but I do not think that, till my turn comes, any human being can make so deep an impression on me.

The priest anointed with holy oil the feet and hands and forehead of the dying woman, repeated a short prayer, and Marguerite was ready to set out for the heaven to which I doubt not she will go, if God has seen the ordeal of her life and the sanctity of her death.

Since then she has not said a word or made a movement. Twenty times I should have thought her dead if I had not heard her breathing painfully.

February 20, 5 *p.m.*

All is over.

Marguerite fell into her last agony at about two o'clock. Never did a martyr suffer such torture, to judge by the cries she uttered. Two or three times she sat upright in the bed, as if she would hold on to her life, which was escaping toward God.

Two or three times also she said your name; then all was silent, and she fell back on the bed exhausted. Silent tears flowed from her eyes, and she was dead.

Then I went up to her; I called her, and as she did not answer I closed her eyes and kissed her on the forehead.

Poor, dear Marguerite, I wish I were a holy woman that my kiss might recommend you to God.

Then I dressed her as she had asked me to do. I went to find a priest at Saint Roch, I burned two candles for her, and I prayed in the church for an hour.

I gave the money she left to the poor.

I do not know much about religion, but I think that God will know that my tears were genuine, my prayers fervent, my alms-giving sincere, and that he will have pity on her who, dying young and beautiful, has only had me to close her eyes and put her in her shroud.

February 22.

The burial took place today. Many of Marguerite's friends came to the church. Some of them wept with sincerity. When the funeral started on the way to Montmartre only two men followed it: the Comte de G., who came from London on purpose, and the duke, who was supported by two footmen.

I write you these details from her house, in the midst of my tears and under the lamp which burns sadly beside a dinner which I can not touch, as you can imagine, but which Nanine has got for me, for I have eaten nothing for twenty-four hours.

My life can not retain these sad impressions for long, for my life is not my own any more than Marguerite's was hers; that is why I give you all these details on the very spot where they occurred, in the fear, if a long time elapsed between them and your return, that I might not be able to give them to you with all their melancholy exactitude.

CHAPTER XXVII

'You have read it?' said Armand, when I finished the manu-
script.

'I understand what you must have suffered, my friend, if all
that I read is true.'

'My father confirmed it in a letter.'

We talked for some time over the sad destiny which had
been accomplished, and I went home to rest a little.

Armand, still sad, but a little relieved by the narration of his
story, soon recovered, and we went together to pay a visit to
Prudence and Julie Duprat.

Prudence had become bankrupt. She told us that Marguerite
was the cause of it; that during her illness she had lent her a lot
of money in the form of promissory notes, which she could
not pay, Marguerite having died without having returned her
the money, and without having given her a receipt with which
she could present herself as creditor.

By the help of the fable, which Mme. Duvernoy repeated
everywhere in order to account for her money difficulties, she
extracted a note for a thousand francs from Armand, who did
not believe it, but who pretended to, out of respect for all
those in whose company Marguerite had lived.

Then we called on Julie Duprat, who told us the sad incident
which she had witnessed, shedding real tears at the remembrance of her friend.

Lastly, we went to Marguerite's grave, on which the first
rays of the April sun were bringing the first leaves into bud.

One duty remained to Armand – to return to his father. He
wished me to accompany him.

We arrived at C., where I saw M. Duval, such as I had
imagined him from the portrait his son had made of him, tall,
dignified, kindly.

He welcomed Armand with tears of joy, and clasped my
hand affectionately. I was not long in seeing that the paternal

sentiment was that which dominated all the others in his mind.

His daughter, named Blanche, had that transparence of eyes, that serenity of mouth, which indicate a soul that conceives only holy thoughts and lips that repeat only pious words. She welcomed her brother's return with smiles, not knowing, in the purity of her youth, that far away a courtesan had sacrificed her own happiness at the mere invocation of her name.

I remained for some time in their happy family, full of indulgent care for one who brought them the convalescence of his heart.

I returned to Paris, where I wrote this story just as it had been told me. It has only one merit, which will perhaps be denied it; that is, that it is true.

I do not draw from this story the conclusion that all women like Marguerite are capable of doing all that she did – far from it; but I have discovered that one of them experienced a serious love in the course of her life, that she suffered for it, and that she died of it. I have told the reader all that I learned. It was my duty.

I am not the apostle of vice, but I would gladly be the echo of noble sorrow wherever I hear its voice in prayer.

The story of Marguerite is an exception, I repeat; had it not been an exception, it would not have been worth the trouble of writing it.